THE LOGIC OF ECONOMICS

This book is dedicated to the gentlemen and scholars of the Ezra L. Koon honor dormitory, Hillsdale College, 1975–78.

THE LOGIC OF ECONOMICS

— and its implications for the public sector

Madsen Pirie, M.A., Ph.D.

Published by
The Adam Smith Institute
1982

First published in 1982 by
The Adam Smith Institute

ISBN 0-906517-16-8

by the same author
TRIAL AND ERROR AND THE IDEA OF PROGRESS, (Open Court, 1978)

Published by the Adam Smith Institute, London SW1
Printed in Great Britain by Butler & Tanner Ltd.
Frome and London

Contents

The Logic of Economics is published by the Adam Smith Institute as a contribution to public debate. The opinions are those of the author and do not necessarily reflect those of the Institute.

Acknowledgements

This book has emerged with the help of many people. For their continual encouragement I should like to thank Stephen Masty and Thomas Farr, both of whom are included already in the general dedication. Eamonn Butler and David Boyd, of the Adam Smith Institute, are both due thanks for their considerable help with the preparation. I am grateful for the very generous help with source materials provided by Chris Tame; and I owe thanks to Timothy Linacre for reading the original draft and making helpful comments. Finally I must thank my long-suffering relatives and friends who put up with me while the book was making its way into the world.

Introduction

The Logic of Economics is a strange title for a book. One expects works dealing with the facts of economics or its methods, but one might wonder what could usefully be said concerning its *logic*.

In much discussion of economics and its problems there is the underlying assumption that its only logic is that which people consciously put into the economic systems which they construct. That kind of logic describes the way in which they try to produce the desired outcome from the various inputs. The undesired or unanticipated happening is taken as a signal that they have got the logic slightly wrong, and need to correct it by an appropriate modification.

In this scheme of things the economic world is treated as a *tabula rasa* on which anything may be written. The institutions and relationships which can be established in economics are seen as limited only by the shortcomings of the imagination. A similar view was once widely held concerning the malleability of human behaviour and relationships. There, too, was the blank slate waiting to be written upon by the intelligent imagination. What might man not become if his nature were reconstructed from his rationality?

There is more caution today concerning the degree to which human nature can be changed by ideas. With the recognition by at least some thinkers that economic activity is the result of purposive human action, there has come more caution in some circles about the degree to which it can be manipulated for desired ends.

The logic with which this book is concerned is that which determines how much we can know about economic activity. By exploring the limitations on knowledge about economic matters, it explores also the limitations on action. Because knowledge is a prerequisite for action, the bounds of what may be known become the bounds of what may be *done*.

Large institutions, especially governments, routinely make policy decisions on the basis of what they suppose to be economic knowledge. Much of the material of this book, and many of its examples, are concerned with the economic activities of government and its institutions, or with the public sector of the economy. Despite the appearance and flavour which this lends to the work, it is as much concerned with philosophy as with economics.

It would have been possible to confine my attentions to showing how logic limits what can be known and done in economics. I have tried to be more constructive, and, even while illustrating how some policy options must be unsuccessful, I have pointed to alternatives which do not violate the logic of economics. An implication of this approach is that the choice between economic policy options is not simply an exercise in the application of taste or political preference. My analysis of the logic leads me to propose instead that some of these policy choices are misconceived, and others simply wrong. I say so now lest the reader be taken unawares.

Numbers

When we use numbers we lose information. The use of numbers depends on our determination to fit things into groups and categories. We might have no use for numbers when considering a hedgehog and an apple, but we certainly would if we were considering an apple and another apple. The concept of 'two apples' presupposes our recognition of similarities.

Numbers have a place in our thinking because we do not perceive the universe as a single, continuous whole. Instead, our senses enable us to break it down into discrete and different objects, according to the different colours, shapes, sounds and smells. It is the similarity, in at least some respects, of these sense impressions, which enables us to use numbers. In using numbers, however, we lose the individuality and uniqueness of the objects we are describing. No apple, for example, is identical to any other apple: we use the term 'two apples' in recognition of some similarities, and in full consciousness that the apples are not identical.

Even at this lowly stage in the use of numbers, when deciding to talk about 'two apples', we have already decided to sacrifice the knowledge that each apple is distinct and individual. We have made a decision which loses this piece of information in order to talk more generally about what they have in common. Each apple has a slightly different shape, weight, size, colour, taste, smell, feel, etc. Yet we have decided to forgo our knowledge about these differences in order to talk about what they have in common. Whatever properties are required to justify our use of the term 'apple' are there; the rest, we have decided, is less important to our purposes.

We can talk, in similar fashion, about 'three pears', losing the information about the unique attributes of each pear, and concentrating instead on what they have in common. We can even override the traditional objections of statisticians and add the three pears to our two apples, arriving at a total of 'five fruit'. We can make the addition by moving to a yet higher stage of generalisation, losing the information that some are apples, some pears, in order to consider them in respect of what they have in common.

The process can be continued. A trout can be added to the apples and pears, making 'six comestibles', even while losing the information that some are fruit and some are fish. Three tables can be added, giving us 'nine objects', and the process can continue even further. At every stage of aggregation, we can increase the numbers by moving to a broader, more general category, and sacrificing yet more information about individual differences.

This loss of information contingent upon the use of numbers creates serious problems for the study of economics. Economic activity is the result of the distinct motivations and decisions of individuals. A decision to buy or not to buy; a preference for more wages instead of more leisure; the determination that it is worth accepting cheaper holidays and a smaller car in order to afford a larger house; these are the reality of economics, and have their origins in human nature.[1] To add different people together and treat them as comparable economic units in spite of their differences in character, temperament and wisdom is to sacrifice detailed information which might be essential for a proper understanding of economic processes.[2]

A physicist is used to dealing with numbers on the large scale. His laws are worded in the form 'whenever a ball is rolled ...', 'if a stone is allowed to fall ...', 'any spring with a weight attached ...'. He is talking about the behaviour of similar objects at a level where the individual differences do not affect the outcome. Although no ball, stone, spring or weight is identical to any other, the physicist talks about behaviour at a level of generality which makes the differences unimportant. A crystallographer, on the other hand, finds that the differences are crucially important at this level, and has to move to a much smaller scale for his generalisations.

When economists talk about such notions as price, demand, or gross national product, they do so in terms which assume that the individual differences between people are insignificant on the scale being considered. Yet there are clearly areas of economics in which the ability to make predictions depends on knowledge of what people are like, and in which the presence of different people will produce a different outcome. In other words, there are levels of economic generalisation in which people do not share the similarities which the physicist can assume for his stones.[3] The key factor is in whether the differences between individuals are on the same scale as the property under consideration. In economics they often are, and thus limit the degree to which aggregation can be taken before unacceptable inaccuracies are incorporated.

Much of economics is directly concerned with information.[4] Price, for example, transmits information impersonally through market mechanisms. Economic behaviour depends upon the information available and how it is perceived, while economic study often records information about how people behaved when choices were presented. Since aggregation involves treating as similar people who are not, and since every stage of generalisation to talk about large numbers involves loss of information from the system under consideration, one has good reason to be sceptical of large-scale treatment of economics.[5]

The logic of aggregation directs us to have diminishing confidence in economic assertions, the greater their distance from the world of individuals motivated to make decisions. A detailed account of the processes which elicit various decisions from farmers, butchers or bureaucrats is less likely to be tainted by unwarranted assumptions than a large-scale treatment of national economic behaviour. In general, the larger the units which are dealt with, the more information will have been lost by the aggregation, and the greater are the errors and inaccuracies incorporated.

The macroeconomic description has already lost in the process of aggregation to the large numbers the very information essential to both the operation and understanding of the system. Microeconomics, on the other hand, confines its consideration to the levels close to individual human action, and manages thereby to retain the information without which no valid account can be attained.

Reality and invention

One problem inherent in the numerical treatment of economics is that in many cases the numbers are applied not to real events and objects, but to man-made concepts related to them. Consider the relationship between heat and temperature. We suppose the heat, that is the excitation of the atoms, to be real. Because we cannot measure this directly, we invent a model we call temperature. Temperature can be measured by the movement of mercury through a tube, or by the rotation of a needle round a scale. It can have numbers attached to it because it is a man-made concept defined in terms of numbers. It is temperature we measure, not heat. The heat, we suppose, is analogous to the temperature we have invented.

In our study of the world around us, including the domain into which human actions intrude, we often have recourse to these man-made concepts in order to quantify. Where we cannot measure the real thing, we invent our analogue which we can measure, and create a model which corresponds with reality sufficient to our purposes. We cannot measure a decline in belief in God, but we can measure a decline in church attendance. We cannot measure the practical nature of early American settlers, but we can record the proportion of the books listed in their wills which were volumes of practical and moral instruction.

Similarly in the study of economics, there are many unmeasurable events alongside of which we can construct indices which we can measure. We might not have access to peoples' minds to determine their state of confidence in the future, but we can measure how much they save, or count the number of ounces of gold they buy. This activity of making our own conceptual models of reality can be instructive, and even rewarding provided that we remember we are dealing with a world of man-made constructs rather than with the real world.

Our economic concepts often stand in for reality. By juggling with them and inspecting the outcome produced from given inputs, we suppose ourselves better able to predict what outcomes will take place in the world of our observation. We do well to keep in mind, however, that our constructs do not describe reality any more than temperature describes heat. It is a mistake to suppose a hypothetical concept devised by us for our convenience must exist in the real world.

The notion of an equilibrium price is one widely used in the study of economics. It is a concept devised by us to illustrate the way in which supply and demand are matched: it represents the result of a convergent process at which the buyers and sellers are matched in the disposal of the available goods. No doubt it is a useful conceptual tool, but no-one should suppose that this equilibrium price, however precise may be the number attached to it, has any existence in the real world of economic exchange. What, for example, is the current equilibrium price for a popular food item? My corner shop is offering 100 gm of a well-known brand of it at £1.35. The same brand is available on the street market one block along at 97p for 100 gm. The local supermarket sells it at £1.05, but offers three different versions of its own brand of the item at prices of 90p, 68p and even 45p for the cheapest. Other supermarkets further afield provide even greater variety. Furthermore, these prices change from day to day and from week to week. What, then, is the equilibrium price?

The answer is that there is none. Equilibrium price is a man-made construct which has no reflection in the everyday world. In the real world, economies do not stop. They continue, ever adapting, ever changing. People on the look-out for opportunity are constantly experimenting with different prices, constantly watching both the level of their sales, and the price of the competition. In the real world there is no balancing point, no time at which the economy can be considered as stationary.[6]

Any indices we devise, or other abstract models we invent to help us to describe an economy are described by us at a point in time, stationary for the moment. They are theoretical efforts to depict the real economy which has the character of a continuing process. As with the river of Heraclitus, we describe, and do not describe, the same economy, for new events are ever flowing about us.

Our determination to apply numbers to the study of economics leads us to juggle with the numbers we attach to our own constructs, and suppose that we are dealing with the actual sizes of real things. This, in turn, leads us to attach more weight to the predictions and explanations generated by the products of our conceptual imagination than they merit. We put inventions into our pot and expect to pull out reality. Economists are noted for their ability to tell us why disasters happened, and for their inability to tell us when they will happen.

False precision

The fallacy of false precision is occasioned when, in attaching exact numbers to imprecise quantities, we allow them to influence us more than their status really merits. If anyone tells us that Frenchmen are 53.6% generous, most of us might assume the figures to be the product of detailed research, and to have some weight in consequence. When we consider how inexact is the term 'generous', and how difficult it would be to measure, we realise that if the figure has any meaning at all — and it may not — it probably represents the score obtained by a small sample of Frenchmen on some index of actions thought by its compiler to be generous. It might even be the result of a score obtained by 200 Frenchmen on a questionnaire, and tell us no more than what 200 Frenchmen said they would do in certain circumstances.[7]

Many economic statistics are found to be as hollow when the process and techniques of measurement are examined. Our nations live or die by statistics. Unemployment rate, gross domestic product, rate of growth, money supply; all are crucial in the determination and judgement of policy. Yet all of them, in one way or another, are difficult to define and difficult to measure.[8] By what processes, for example, does the civil service arrive at a measure of the rate of growth of the economy? It is a subtraction of two figures for gross domestic product, which is supposed to represent the sum of all of the economic activity which is taking place in the nation. A wife at home who draws housekeeping money from her husband is not included in GDP. If, however, the marriage breaks up, as they often do, and they part on amicable terms, which happens more rarely, the husband may decide to employ his ex-wife as a housekeeper, paying her the same as before. The difference is that her efforts are now included in GDP.

Even aside from the difficulties of determining what does or does not count as productive activity, the ability of civil servants to collect accurate figures on what they do agree on is highly questionable. Estimates of the error margin vary. I would be surprised if they could collect even the figure they were looking for to an accurancy level with ± 10%. Less sceptical observers suggest ± 5%. Even if we take the accuracy to be within 3% of what they are trying to measure, whether or not that means anything, we can see the potential error in a figure for growth rate.

A growth rate announced at 1% by subtracting this year's figure for GDP from last year's, each subject to a ± 3%, could be a growth rate of 7%, or a recession rate of 5%. Yet these are the figures on which policy is determined. To this vast range of possible findings we can add firstly the uncertainty of whether the civil servants have included the correct things in their tables, and secondly the risk of falsification. The 'black' economy, which takes place below the official statistics, may be as high as 20%, instead of the more conventional 7% normally ascribed to it. If people are not telling civil servants details of their real economic performance, the official figures lose more credibility.[9]

This can present genuine problems. Consider the case of a government attempting to control inflation by a squeeze on the supply of money. In this hypothetical case, let us suppose that the level of unemployment rises as was predicted. Let us further add that the rate of business bankruptcies increased as expected, and that prices came down more or less within a few percent of their target levels. There are a few other indicators we can add, all of which we shall suppose to be in the range which a monetary squeeze might produce. Now let us add that the money supply figures show a complete failure on the part of government to control them. The statistics, in our fanciful case, show money supply exceeding the government target every month. What are we to believe?[10]

Those with a faith in economic numbers might opt for the money supply figures indicating money to be out of control. Unfortunately, this involves them in abandoning their faith in the other numbers relating to unemployment, bankruptcies, etc. Sceptics might opt for the explanation that the measurement of money supply is wrong, on the grounds that factors such as the number out of jobs, the number of firms which close, and so on, are easy to understand and to measure, whereas there is considerable conceptual difficulty in deciding what money is and how it can be measured. Yet another group might accept all of the figures and claim that they showed inflation could be controlled without a monetary squeeze. A final group of economic nihilists might reject all of the figures as dealing with factors improperly conceptualised, inadequately defined, and imperfectly measured. All are possible: the problem lies in deciding which to prefer.

Further complications arise because the use of numbers applied to economic concepts creates confusion between those which are real events, quantified insofar as we can by numerical indices, and those which are determined by the product or outcome of economic reality. The blurred distinction between inputs and outcomes can lead to tragic failures in policy. It is widely believed, for example, that governments can legislate to control wages and prices. By restraining these with legal authority, it is argued, government can hold down the cost of labour and component goods, thus controlling output prices. Thus comes about the belief in prices and incomes policy as a means of limiting inflation.

The reasoning is faulty. The numbers attached to wages and prices are recording the *results* of economic activity. The real events of economics, the desires of individuals to better themselves and provide more for their families, and the decisions taken in the light of those desires, these are what cause wages and prices to assume their measured levels. The ratio between the supply of goods and services, including labour, which results from the play of those real factors, and the demand for those goods and services which results from similar forces, go to make up the wages and prices which are recorded. Governments may legislate artificial levels unless they work on the real factors which produce them. The legislated levels, therefore, cause shortages in supply (since they are invariably held down rather than up), and push the real levels into the hiding-place of the black market.[11]

Indeed, almost any interference with the numbers from the legislative end will send false signals radiating through the economy. The numbers which normally convey information will transmit falsehood instead, and will lead people into decisions they would never have made with correct information. Thus comes about the over-expansion of production industry, the taking on of too many employees, the borrowing of more money than the market justifies, and all of the other mistakes into which people are led by false numbers.[12]

The money supply

Some governments have attempted to control inflation and regulate the economy back into health by maintaining a firm intention to hold down the rate of increase in the supply of money. The belief underpinning this policy is that the quantity of money is a prime determinant of economic outcome, and that if the money is held down at the top, the factors underneath will be required to sort themselves within the tyranny of its limits.

There is a trivial sense it which it is true that 'inflation is always and everywhere a monetary phenomenon'. The lowering of the purchasing power of money has been accompanied by an increase in the supply of it, exceeding any increase in the production of goods and services. Similarly, the steadying of money's buying power has witnessed as its companion the cessation of that surplus of supply. It is a simple *cum hoc ergo propter hoc* to draw a causal link from this simultaneity.

The figure for the total quantity of money is an aggregate, representing the result of many, many economic realities. It is determined by real economic activity, and can be altered by altering the real economic activity. If the attempt is made to hold down the quantity of money, without attacking the source and origin of its determination, the attempt will not succeed. If those factors, in other words, which cause money supply to expand remain unaltered and still producing their effects, then they will defeat the attempt of government to hold down the overall figure.[13]

Some of the factors which inflate money supply take the form of pressures on government. To leave those pressures in place, despite a nominal commitment to restraint, is to set reality to work against desire. The public sector of the economy has forces which lead governments to expand the money supply; and those forces will still exert that pressure unless they are tackled. To suppose that government can hold to a mere intention, when real forces are working on it, is to place desire above reality. The institutional and political pressures exerted on government by the public sector will cause the arbitrary limits on money supply to be broken.

The roots of inflation are firmly anchored in government expenditure and the factors which push it upward. The immunity of public sector production of goods and services to ordinary market disciplines, the tendency of public sector operations to be captured by the producers, both administrators and labour force, the vulnerability of government to certain public sector unions enjoying immense legal powers; all of these put pressure on government to increase its spending. Unless the pressures themselves are dealt with, no-one should be surprised to witness a failure on the part of government to hold money supply within preordained limits. Economic reality will out, and if government requires too large a helping of money, more of it will be produced.

Understanding the pattern

Examination of the role of numbers in economics can lead to a profound and healthy skepticism concerning what types of thing may be known. Certainly, much of what passes for general knowledge in modern economics seems to bear more of the character of a perpetually modified history than of a series of repeatable laws.

In a typical scenario, economists advise government, and the expected outcome fails to materialise. The economists explain, afterwards, of course, the special factors which altered the outcome of the general expectation. This happens again, and again the general rule has more special exceptions incorporated. Added together, the explanation which suffices to explain economic history becomes as long as the history itself, since every outcome requires special attention. All of this could be another way of saying that economic events are unique, and not susceptible of general explanation.[14]

History, which is admittedly composed of unique events, appeals for its explanatory power to general knowledge of human nature, and our general awareness that some patterns are repeated in form if not in detail. There are some historical laws, but they hold nothing like the force of scientific laws, nor are they accompanied by the expectation that the behaviour will indeed be repeated at each new test. It could be that history, dealing as it does with human action, has the raw material of its study on such a scale that individual differences are large enough to intrude into the area of study.

The study of economics can learn much from its older and more illustrious professional colleague. History attempts less, seeming more aware of its limitations. Few indeed are the historians who sit at the right hand of policy-makers to utter *ex cathedra* pronouncements about the future.

There are, as we have seen, generalisations in economics which, like those of history, have their origins in human nature and the action which it impels. On the larger scale, there are undoubtedly generalisations which tell us about the pattern of events. The physicist at the nuclear level can make statistical predictions, even though he might be unable to gain access to what it is that causes individual particles to act as they do. Similarly the economist might, by dealing with large numbers, fill in the outline or pattern of what is taking place, though he, too, lacks knowledge of the behaviour of individuals. In this way he can outline for us the form of events, if not the detail.

It is instructive to proceed from a few empirical observations about economic activity to a determination of some of the factors which must be included before any account can be successful. Let us look briefly at a typical operation of the market. A tin mine ceases to produce, thus lowering the supply of tin on the market. No-one need know why; indeed, no-one need even know it has happened. With a reduced supply, and an unchanged demand, sellers can get more money for their tin, and do so. The rise in price shows the market as a vehicle for more information than any individual has access to. Because people wish to maximise their advantage, they use less tin if they can. They turn to cheaper substitutes if there are any, perhaps ones which were just dearer than tin at the old price, and are now cheaper. Meanwhile, previously uneconomic tin mines can now be brought into production by those who see a chance of making money by doing so. The effect is thus to encourage people to consume less tin, while encouraging them to produce more.

Without considering the ecological implications which the market has,[15] we can see several important elements in this example. Firstly, we can see the market as a mechanism which acts to preserve its function. The market resulted in a shortage of tin being met with a response which overcame the shortage. It acted not in a way which preserved the *status quo*, as a thermostat acts, but in a way which took it into a new situation. Far from acting as a homeostatic system, which keeps itself the same, the market acted dynamically in a way which preserved its function by producing a new distribution of the available supply, and by prompting new supply.

Secondly, we can see that the motive force behind the actual operation of the market's mechanisms is the desire of individuals to better their lot.[16] It is because sellers stood to gain that the price went up, and because buyers wished to do better that they bought substitutes at a lower price. It was because people wanted to make money that tin was mined in new areas. All of these human actions show us human purposes as the market's driving force.

These empirical observations show us that no account of economic operations will be successful unless it depicts the market as a *process*, rather than as a set state of affairs.[17] The market's continuous function creates constantly changing realities, and any description will recognize this. We can see also that any successful depiction of the economic process must have its origins in human action. Any account which fails to admit human motivation, and to allow for the way in which individuals make decisions from a desire to improve their lot, will fall short of the task of explanation.[18]

A further observation we can make from our consideration is that, since the market is a transmitter of information, and since that information is essential to its operation, then we require an account which retains as much of that information as possible. The more information we lose from our account, the less adequately will it tell us about the market as it really operates in each case.

It has already been established that information is lost at each stage of aggregation, that each time we increase the numbers talked about, we lose further information about individual differences.

Thus we can add to our requirements of any economic explanation that it shall not deal with large-scale aggregate units, but with the detail of individual cases.

Many other factors are doubtless required of economic explanations, but the foregoing establishes that they must fulfil those three requirements at the very least. All of them are limitations on our proposed explanations; none of them tells us anything about the content. Logic usually tells us what we cannot do: it rules out certain combinations and tells us that if some things are true, then others must be false. Logic, used correctly, will never give us information about the universe. All it can do is enable us to process our inputs in such a way that we can specifically reject certain arrangements of them. It cannot give us the inputs, nor tell us if they are true or false.

Starting with a few inputs derived from the world of our observation, the logic of economics leads us to stipulate three requirements, or minimum conditions, of explanation, and shows us that accounts which fail to comply with them must be numbered among the impermissible combinations. This is not to say that all explanations in compliance must be valid; only that those which do not comply must be less than satisfactory. Proposed explanations must:

1. Treat the market as a process rather than as a state of affairs or a series of discrete events;
2. Have the origins of its operating forces rooted in the self-motivated behaviour of individuals;
3. Avoid high levels of generality (macroeconomics) which lose information essential to the operation and understanding of the system.

As an example of an explanation which meets these requirements, we might consider one which has been advanced to add insight to the relationship between government, money and inflation. A crude notion, to be rejected, stipulates that government introduces new money into the economy, over and above any increase in production. Following a time lag, which varies from one month to two years, there is a general price rise corresponding to the level of increase of the money supply.

The explanation we look at now is crucially different. It points out that new money is not introduced into the economy like icing spread all over the surface of a cake, but enters at a particular point.

It is introduced by government in the form of cash or credit for the purchase of producer goods. Producer goods industries, being nearest to the new money, receive its signals first and strongest. It sends them false signals of a higher demand, and they expand output accordingly. An increase in the supply of credit makes money seem cheaper to borrow, and misinforms producers about the real cost of capital investment. Resources are committed to the production of capital goods, when there has been no shift in real demand. And so the new money works its way through the economy, with each sector responding in turn to its signals. The signals were false, however, expressing not real demand, but artificial input by government. On the assumption that government cannot keep doing this indefinitely, in ever-increasing amounts, the process must be stopped at some stage. There will be, by then, a vast surplus of over-capacity in producer industries, a surplus which must be shaken out in recession and unemployment. The longer the process of monetary inflation has continued, the greater will need to be the readjustment to economic reality.

The explanation has been more than adequately covered in economic literature: it suffices for our purposes to inspect its characteristics.[19] Firstly, it is an account which treats the economy as a continuing process, and which attempts to follow inputs through the workings of the system which it describes. It is therefore in accord with the first of our requirements.

Secondly, it traces the consequences of those inputs through the responses which are made by business firms and single individuals. Receiving signals which indicate increase in demand, they see opportunities to expand, and do so to generate more business and more profit. Entrepreneurs provide the means by which economic responses are elicited by inputs. The system, in other words, depends upon human motivation and action, as is required by our second condition.

As for the third requirement, we can see that instead of talking in broad aggregate terms about such things as 'a 10% increase in money supply', or a 'general price rise of 10%', this explanation looks at individuals who first receive the new money, and examines their response. It operates on a scale which retains the detailed and individual information lost in larger and more general accounts. This account of monetary inflation is therefore more satisfactory than the crude notion which was couched in such sweeping terms, and which therefore lacked the essential detail to fill in a clear picture of the process.

It would be no bad thing if other large-scale purported accounts of economic affairs were subjected to the same test. Some would undoubtedly fail, but many would survive by going into more detail. By examining the economy as a process in the same remorseless detail, they would find the extra information that would enrich and enhance their explanatory power. By remaining closer to the individual, and watching him respond in the various stages of a continuing process, they would tell us something about the real world, the world in which economic activity takes place. By attempting less, they would achieve more.

FOOTNOTES

1. The philosophical literature on the importance of individual consciousness and decision-making behind human events deals mostly with historical explanations, but it is still highly relevant to students of economics, both disciplines being concerned with human action. The German scholar, Wilhelm Dilthey, argued that the distinguishing methodology of the human studies 'went beyond the external perception of nature ... to the internal states which lay beyond their experiences'. For a discussion of Dilthey's philosophy see Gordon Leff, *History and Social Theory*, Merlin Press, London 1969, p. 28 ff. See also in regard to these methodological issues R. G. Collingwood, *An Autobiography*, Oxford University Press, London, 1970, especially Chapter X.

2. For an excellent statement of the primacy of individuals in the human 'sciences', see Gordon Leff, *op cit*, especially Part I, Chapter III. See also J. W. N. Watkins, 'Methodological Individualism and Social Tendencies', in May Brodbeck, ed., *Readings in the Philosophy of the Social Sciences*, Macmillan, New York, 1968.

3. For a readable and brief critique of 'scientism', i.e., the use of methods appropriate only to the physical sciences in the study of man, see Murray N. Rothbard, 'The Mantle of Science', in H. Schoeck and J. W. Wiggins, eds, *Scientism and Values*, D. Van Nostrand, Princeton, New Jersey, 1960. And, of course, F. A. Hayek, *The Counter Revolution of Science*, Allen and Unwin, London, 1952.

4. It is largely the 'Austrian School' of economics, and specifically the contributions of F. A. Hayek, which stresses this view of economics and explains its significance. See especially 'Economics and Knowledge' and 'The Use of Knowledge in Society', in F. A. Hayek, *Individualism and*

Economic Order, Routledge and Kegan Paul, London, 1949, and 'Competition as a Discovery Procedure', in Hayek, *New Studies in Philosophy, Politics, Economics, and the History of Ideas*, Routledge and Kegan Paul, London, 1978. For a useful introduction to Hayek's work see G. P. O'Driscoll, Jr, *Economics as a Coordination Problem: The Contribution of F. A. Hayek*, Sheed, Andrews and McMeel, Kansas City, 1977. For recent developments of this approach see Israel Kirzner, *Competition and Entrepreneurship*, University of Chicago Press, 1973 (especially pp. 227–231 on entrepreneurship and information); *Idem*, *Perception, Opportunity and Profit*. University of Chicago Press, 1979; and Thomas Sowell, *Knowledge and Decisions*, Basic Books, New York, 1980.

5. See Ludwig M. Lachman, 'Toward a Critique of Macroeconomics', in E. G. Dolan, ed., *The Foundations of Modern Austrian Economics*, Sheed, Andrews and McMeel, Kansas City, 1976; *Idem*, *Macro-economic thinking and the Market Economy: An Essay on the Neglect of the Micro-Foundations and its Consequences*, Institute of Economic Affairs, London, 1973; L. M. Spadaro, 'Averages and Aggregates in Economics', in M. Sennholz, ed., *On Freedom and Free Enterprise*. D. Van Nostrand, Princeton, New Jersey, 1956: F. A. Hayek, 'The Misuse of Aggregates', in S. Shenoy, ed., *A Tiger by the Tail: The Keynesian Legacy of Inflation*, Institute of Economic Affairs, London, 2nd edn, 1978, pp. 13–22; Ludwig Von Mises, 'The Approach of Macroeconomics', in his *The Ultimate Foundation of Economic Science*, D. Van Nostrand, Princeton, New Jersey, 1962, pp. 83–87. This does not say, of course, that a soundly micro-based macro-economics might not be elaborated. See R. W. Garrison, *Austrian Macroeconomics: A Diagrammatical Exposition*, Institute for Humane Studies, Menlo Park, California, 1978.

6. See, in this respect, Ludwig Von Mises, *Human Action: A Treatise on Economics*, William Hodge, London, 1945, pp. 245–251; also see pp. 237–238 on 'The Method of Imaginary Constructions'. As Von Mises said, although indispensable in economic reasoning, such 'imaginary constructions' can cause one to fall into a 'chasm of absurdity and nonsense'. In much economics pertaining to 'equilibrium' and 'perfect competition' they clearly have.

7. For a witty exposure of the nonsense inherent in so much social science quantification see Stanislav Andreski, *Social Sciences as Sorcery*, Penguin Books, Harmondsworth, Middlesex, 1974, esp. chapter 10, 'Quantification as Camouflage', pp. 130–151, see also W. W. Sharrock, 'Some Problems with Social Research', in A. Seldon, ed., *Town Hall Power or Whitehall Pawn?*, Institute of Economic Affairs, London, 1980.

8. See, for example, Oskar Morgernstern, *On the Accuracy of Economic Observations*, Princeton University Press, New Jersey, 2nd edn, 1963; the section on national income statistics in this work has also been recently

reprinted as a separate monograph, *Idem*, *National Income Statistics: A Critique of Macroeconomic Aggregation*, Cato Institute, San Francisco, 1979; see also Roger LeRoy Miller, *The Economics of Macro Issues*, Harper and Row, New York, 1978, esp. chapter 6 'The Economics of Measuring GNP', pp. 27–30 and chapter 8 'The Economics of Measuring Unemployment', pp. 34–39. Also, on the difficulties of measuring unemployment see John B. Wood, *How Little Unemployment?*, Institute of Economic Affairs, London, 1975, *Idem*, *How Much Unemployment? The Methods and Measures Dissected*, Institute of Economic Affairs, London, 1972. On the measurement of inequality, see *Idem*, *How Much Inequality? An Inquiry into the Evidence*, Institute of Economic Affairs, London, 1974; on measuring money supply, see Robert Miller, 'Measuring the Money Supply', *International Currency Review*, Vol. 9, No. 3, 1977, and *Measuring Money: The Inadequacy of the Present Tools*, Centre for Policy Studies, London, 1981.

9. See Graeme Shankland, *Our Secret Economy*, Anglo-German Foundation. For the Study of Industrial Society, London, 1980. Also see J. I. Gershuny and R. E. Pahl, 'Britain in the Decade of the Three Economies', *New Society*, 3 January 1980; J. Walmsley, 'The Booming Black Economy', *Evening Standard*, 17 March 1980; J. I. Gershuny, 'The More Cheerful Informal Economy', the *Financial Times*, 9 August 1979; G. Hawtin, 'Black is Profitable', the *Financial Times*, 7 June 1978; R. Junor, 'Britain's Black Economy', the *Daily Telegraph*, 25 June 1979; on the black economy in Italy see D. Lane, 'There's No Black Comedy in the Italians "Moonlighting",' the *Guardian*, 4 April 1979; On Sweden see R. Junor, 'Friday — A National Day for Moonlighting', the *Daily Telegraph*, 10 July 1979; On Russia see C. Hershfeld, 'Purple Jeans and the Unplanned Economy', *Socialist Worker*, 23 June 1979. On Hungary, see János Kenedi, *Do it Yourself: Hungary's Hidden Economy*, Pluto Press, London, 1981. For a theoretical analysis see Max Thurn, 'The Underground Economy', and Barbara Shenfield 'Comment', papers delivered at the Mont Pelerin Society Meeting, Stanford, California, 1980.

10. This underlines the deficiencies of crude measurement manifest in some so-called 'positive' economics, the severance of fundamental reasoning from empirical testing. See Mario J. Rizzo, 'Praxeology and Econometrics: A Critique of Positive Economics', in L. M. Spadaro, *New Directions in Austrian Economics*, Sheed, Andrews and McMeel, Kansas City, 1978. See also, H. F. Sennholz, 'Chicago Monetary Tradition in the Light of Austrian Theory', in F. A. Hayek, et al, *Toward Liberty*, Institute for Humane Studies, Menlo Park, California, 1972, Vol. 2. That 'Chicago School' economics is freer of such crudity than is much mainstream neoclassical work is probably true, however. See Alan C. Reynolds, 'The Purge of Chicago Economists', *Reason*, Vol. 3, No. 1, July 1971 and *Idem*,

'Economics, Ethics and Epistemology', *Reason*, Vol. 3, No. 11, February 1972.

11. On prices and incomes legislation see M. Walker, ed., *The Illusion of Wage and Price Control*, Fraser Institute, Vancouver, 1976; R. L. Schuettinger, *A Brief Survey of Price & Wage Controls from 2800 B.C. to A.D. 1953*, Heritage Foundation, Washington, D.C., 1974; and the definitive study by Eamonn F. Butler & R. L. Schuettinger, *Forty Centuries of Wage and Price Controls*, Heritage Foundation, Washington, D.C., 1979.

12. This is, in a nutshell, the 'Austrian Theory' of the Trade Cycle. See F. A. Hayek, *Monetary Theory and the Trade Cycle*, Routledge and Kegan Paul, London, 1933, *Idem*, *Prices and Production*, Routledge and Kegan Paul, London, 2nd edn, 1935; Ludwig Von Mises, *The Theory of Money and Credit*, Yale University Press, 1959; *Idem*, et al, *The Austrian Theory of the Trade Cycle and Other Essays*, Centre for Libertarian Studies, New York, 1979; Lionel Robbins, *The Great Depression*, Macmillan, London, 1934; Murray N. Rothbard, *America's Great Depression*, Sheed, Andrews and McMeel, Kansas City, 3rd edn, 1975; Ludwig Lachman, *Capital and its Structure*, Sheed, Andrews and McMeel, Kansas City, 1978.

13. See A. Seldon, ed., *Is Monetarism Enough?*, Institute of Economic Affairs, London, 1980; R. Bacon et al, *The Dilemmas of Government Expenditure*, I.E.A., London, 1976; S. Littlechild et al, *The Taming of Government*, I.E.A., London, 1979; R. J. Gordon, 'The Demand for and Supply of Inflation', *The Journal of Law and Economics*, Vol. XVIII, No. 3, December 1975.

14. Which is largely what the German 'Historical School' of Economics held. It was against such views that the Austrian School elaborated its contrary position. See C. Gide and C. Rist, *A History of Economic Doctrines*, George C. Harrap, London, 1915, pp. 379–407. And see also Eugen Von Böhm-Bawerk, 'The Historical vs. the Deductive Method in Political Economy', *Annals of the American Academy of Political and Social Science*, Vol. 1, No. 2, October 1890.

15. A useful introductory text on this topic is E. G. Dolan, *TANSTAAFL: The Economic Strategy For Environmental Crisis*, Holt, Rinehart and Winston, New York, 1971; *Idem*, 'Environmental Policy and Property Rights'; in S. L. Blumenfeld, ed., *Property in a Humane Economy*, Open Court, La Salle, Illinois, 1974; Murray N. Rothbard, 'Conservation and the Free Market', in his *Egalitarianism As A Result Against Nature and Other Essays*, Libertarian Review Press, Washington, D.C., 1974; R. Poole Jr, 'Reason and Ecology', in D. B. James, ed., *Outside Looking In*, Harper and Row, New York, 1972; L. E. Ruff, 'The Economic Common Sense of Pollution', *The Public Interest*, No. 19, Spring 1970.

16. This should not be confused with vulgar concepts of 'selfishness' or

the so-called 'economic man'. See Philip H. Wicksteed, *The Common Sense of Political Economy*, Vol. 1, Routledge and Kegan Paul, London, 1935, especially chapter 5, 'Business and the Economic Nexus', pp. 158–211. See also Israel M. Kirzner, *The Economic Point of View*, D. Van Nostrand, Princeton, New Jersey, 1960, *passim*.

17. Indeed, one Austrian School economist, Walter Grinder, has suggested that the term 'Austrian (School) Economics would be better, and less ambiguously, served by the term the 'process school'. See also the essays by Israel Kirzner, 'On the Central Concept of Austrian Economics: Market Process', and 'Equilibrium versus Market Process', in E. G. Dolan, ed., *The Foundations of Modern Austrian Economics*, op cit. The policy relevance of this approach is demonstrated clearly in Kirzner's monograph, *The Perils of Regulation: A Market-Process Approach*, Law and Economics Centre Occasional Paper, University of Miami School of Law, Coral Gates, Florida, 1978.

18. On the specific principle of methodological individualism, see Ludwig Von Mises, 'The Principle of Methodological Individualism', in his *Human Action*, op. cit., pp. 41–43; and *Idem*, 'The Climate of Economic Science', op. cit., pp. 80–83; Ludwig Lachman, 'Methodological Individualism and the Market Process', in his *Capital*, *Expectations and the Market Process*, Sheed, Andrews and McMeel, Kansas City, 1977. On the broader relevance of the principle in the humane studies see the essays by J. W. N. Watkins, in J. O'Neill, ed., *Modes of Individualism and Collectivism*, Heinemann, London, 1973, and Chris R. Tame, 'Man, Concepts and Society', in *Wertfrei*, No. 2, Spring 1974.

19. As well as the works cited in footnote 11 of this chapter see also Lachman, *Capital*, *Expectations and the Market Process*, op. cit.

The costs of government

It is a common mistake to suppose that because government provides so expensive a service, its costs may be cut. Few who contemplate the figures fail to be appalled by the high administrative cost and low output of government departments and programmes. From time to time experts from the world of private business are brought in as consultants, to weed out some of the practices and procedures which would never be tolerated in private enterprise. Reorganisations, amalgamations and shake-ups take place, and government settles down again after some time into its established routine.[1]

The point is, of course, that government is not subject to the ordinary commercial pressures which keep overhead costs low and promote efficiency. Government enjoys a protected and privileged position, and does not normally risk losing the trade to a leaner, fitter competitor, or of going bankrupt. In the absence of private sector disciplines imposed on costs and practices, the operation of government is dominated by other factors.

There are forces at work on the operation of government, even though these are not the ones to be found at work in the business world. The activity of government, like the activity of business, is made up of the actions of individuals in pursuit of aims, and limited or channelled in their efforts by the circumstances which prevail, or the rules which are imposed upon them. The circumstances and rules which direct the individuals in government are not the same as those which constrain in business activity, but their role as determinants is none the less valid.[2]

The imposition upon government, from time to time, of some of the practices characteristic of the world of business enterprise only creates an artifical and temporary situation. To achieve lasting success, the rules and circumstances would have to be changed to such an extent that the activity was barely recognisable any longer as government. The activity of attempting to bring government up to commercial standards of productivity and efficiency by the adoption of businesslike methods reminds one irresistibly of those communist societies which allow a small market to operate somewhere, in order that the giant planned economy may learn from it the 'real' price of goods.

From time to time there are more sustained and large-scale efforts to cut the cost of government. As more and more programmes are undertaken by government, more and more services provided, and more and more industries fall within the public sector, then the greater is the burden which falls on the productive part of society. Government, to finance its operations, can pre-empt in taxation the money which would otherwise be available to finance investment in the renewal and expansion of private business. The need to pay for government can leave people unable to pay for the products of the private, wealth-generating, sector, and can create a serious shortage of effective demand to sustain it.

It has been suggested that with high levels of taxation, people will work more in order to maintain their standard of living.[3] The contrary is true. Leisure has its price, like other things, and is cheap when only a little money would be earned if the time were spent in work. It is when taxes are low, and high earnings have to be forgone for leisure that it becomes expensive.[4] With high taxes, leisure is cheaper, and people consume more of it. There is less incentive to work, so the economic base declines. High cost government, in other words, tends to reduce economic activity.

It is scarcely surprising in view of the adverse consequences of high cost government, that reforming administrations should be elected occasionally on a platform of making major cutbacks in the size and cost of government. What is more surprising is that they are almost never successful in their attempts to do so.

Typically, a cost-cutting administration will announce a package of cuts shortly after it assumes office. Administrative detail and procedure delays some, and others are delayed while protests are heard, or ameliorated in response to powerful interest group pressure. Surprised, and perhaps somewhat irked to see how little was achieved, the administration proposes a new round of savings for the following year. But it has already selected the obvious, less popular targets for its first round; so there is even more resistance to the second list. By the time the third list of cutbacks is produced, the next election looms on the horizon, and there is no serious chance of any real success.

Under the Conservative government elected in 1979 on a programme to cut the cost of government, the cost increased every year, and the proportion of the economy occupied by the public sector increased every year. Economy campaigns in the United States at about the same time similarly failed to decrease the cost of government.[5]

Cutting the fat

The reasons for the failure become more evident when examination is made of the methods used. The attempt is to cut 'inefficiency and wastage', rather than any benefits conveyed by the operations of government. The 'fat' of overhigh costs on manpower, administration and paperwork is targeted for savings, rather than the 'lean meat' of actual services and programmes. The assumption is made that tighter and more economical control can result in a saving in costs without loss of activity.

Ministers who ask their departments to locate unnecessary and wasteful work in order that it might be cut are not usually trampled to death in the rush. The career structure of the administration rewards more responsibility with a higher pay and status. The incentive for the bureaucrat is to increase, rather than diminish, the work done within his department. If civil service activity were simply treated as business, and administrators were assumed to behave not as selfless public servants, but as normal people attempting to maximise their advantage within the prevailing rules and circumstances, we would have a reasonable model to account for their behaviour.

They attempt, so far as is possible, to increase their share of the 'business' activity, that is, to increase the area of their concerns and responsibilities. Just as a company, squeezed out of one market, will try to make inroads into another, so will a civil service department threatened with the loss of one function acquire new involvements and areas of concern. Just as a company will cultivate a brand image to ensure that its product is recognised as distinctive, meeting a specific need, so will a civil service department attempt to establish that its own activities are uniquely necessary, and will go to great lengths to render them distinctive, and show they do not overlap with or duplicate the work of other departments.

A business concern, faced with the need to make economies, is hardly likely to find section heads volunteering that their departments are over-manned, inefficient, and suitable candidates for the axe, even though there is the incentive to find the savings in order that the company, including the jobs of the section heads, will survive. A civil service department, without even the incentive to ensure overall survival, is even less likely to volunteer itself as victim for an economy campaign. Even the cabinet minister at the top has his importance judged by the size of his department and the scope of its activities. He, too, is unlikely to volunteer to make himself less important.

Armed with previous experience of this perfectly predictable behaviour, some government attempts to cut public sector costs have favoured cash limits, or controls on the overall budget, ministry by ministry. The idea has been that under the shadow of a total cash limit on spending, economies would be forced where they could most easily be made. Failure to economise in one section affects the budget of others, and therefore incurs their opposition. So, runs the theory, savings will be made where least impact results, and that will be on the fat of administration rather than on the meat of service.

What happens in practice is that the savings are proposed in the most sensitive areas of service. Political opposition is maximised. The government retreats from its original intent under a hail of criticism. Even after proceeding resolutely ahead with some of the proposals, the government nonetheless finds at the end of the year that spending has been higher than that dictated by the cash limits.

The structure of public service dictates the outcome. Although the decisions are made by legislators, they have to be implemented by administration officials. These officials know quite well how vulnerable legislators are to political and popular pressure. Asked to implement savings, the administrators produce proposals which will result in the curtailing of the most popular part of the service. The media, gaining the story either officially or unofficially, highlight the threat, and public and political opinion is mobilised against the plan.

It is a very resolute legislator indeed who can withstand this pressure without at least moderating the stringency of the economy campaign. The result of this is that while no desk job or filing clerk's position is put at risk, or suggested as a possible saving, proposals are put forward by the departments which would have the effect of closing hospitals for crippled children, or throwing old people out onto the streets.

The overall spending by each department should be seen more as the product of the activities which take place within it, rather than as the determinant of those activities. In other words, the institutional procedures and operations of all of the sections within a department have their outcome in an overall spending figure. To limit that figure in the attempt to control the activities which result in it is to tackle the problem the wrong way round. If the activities which lead to high spending are put in order, then the outcome will be a lower spending figure. If the attempt is made to control that figure while leaving unchecked the forces which cause it to rise, then spending will burst the bonds which are set upon it.

Cutting the programmes

It might be thought that real savings could be effected, and cash limits complied with, if instead of attempting to trim programme costs by saving 'fat' from their administration, whole programmes were entirely eliminated. After all, one could surely expect that some programmes were not reaching their intended target, that some had been rendered out of date by social advances, or that some had costs out of all proportion to any benefits dispensed.

The problem is that while all of these assumptions may be true,[6] there is scarcely a state programme without its coterie of beneficiaries. And while those who benefit perceive their gain as large, those who lose — the general taxpayers — perceive their loss from each programme as small. Every activity of government therefore has a group prepared to defend it more strongly than others are prepared to attack it.[7]

Numbers are of little consequence. The small number who defend the programme are more visible to the media than the large numbers who are hostile. The hostility, moreover, is lukewarm, whereas the defence is passionate. Any programme whatsoever can therefore be expected to result in scenes of hardship in the media to illustrate the consequences of its demise. The bureaucrats whose jobs are at risk will co-operate willingly with beneficiary groups and dramatising journalists. No matter how useless the programme, how ineffective it has been, or how little of its benefits reach their target, any administration which proposes to terminate it will face a barrage of hostility and be depicted as if they were numbered among the most hard-hearted of Victorian landlords. Legislators, disliking this presentation of them, soon learn to minimise the activity which prompts it.

Any government which embarks on a systematic elimination of superfluous and expensive programmes, soon finds that it is able to achieve only a small part of the public sector reduction which it intended. Its first list, moreover, contained all of the most obvious candidates for the axe; any subsequent list drawn up to make good the failure to achieve success in the first round, will necessarily be composed of programmes deemed more worthy to survive than the first group. Opposition to their elimination will be even more intense, especially in the light of its success in tempering the first wave of cuts.

One can predict with inexorable logic that a government engaged in the reduction of public sector programmes will encounter ever increasing political opposition in return for ever diminishing savings. Eventually, and for most governments sooner rather than later, the administration will prefer to end the protests and the unpopularity engendered by reaction to its policies, reckoning correctly that the savings it does manage to achieve are bought at too high a price.

Public sector generalisation

The only area of public sector spending in which results can be gained at comparatively low costs lies on the capital side of the account. Since current spending has all of the internal forces lined up behind it, it is a major struggle to achieve economies there. Both in administrative 'fat' and the 'meat' of the programmes, the structure is one which militates in favour of a status quo of sustained expansion. With salary increases to be paid, and the expectation that benefits will not fall in real terms, there is constant pressure on the current account to sustain regular increases simply to keep things as they are. Any administration attempting economies faces a major battle to prevent the costs from increasing every year, even before it can spare any thought or effort towards their reduction.

The capital side, however, represents future programmes. Expectations are lower for promised joy; and a government can postpone the arrival of tomorrow's jam more readily than it can remove today's from the plate. The delay or abandonment of future improvements does not bear immediate consequences to most people. The prospect of waiting yet another year is easier to sell than the diminution of gains already received. Naturally enough, in view of the political pressures which a government faces, it is always the capital projects which bear the brunt of economy campaigns.[8]

Pictures on television of an empty field where hypothetical children will one day attend a future school make less dramatic presentations than pictures of the children whose school is to be closed, or of the worried parents who fight to keep it open. The capital side is less sensitive to media pressure, and is therefore the soft option. The jobs lost by deferment of capital investment are less easy to see than those put at risk by current account saving. And they certainly cause less trouble.

Inspection of periods when reforming adminstrations have succeeded in making inroads into public sector costs shows a one-sided attack on the capital account. Such savings are temporary; at some stage the capital has to be topped up. Roads may break up, hospital queues lengthen, traffic delays mount. At some time action has to be taken to restore the capital depleted by the saving. Governments hope, of course, that while savings have been made in times of hardship, they can be restored in a time of economic plenty: so does everyone who mortgages the future for present consumption.

Three rather surprising hypotheses may be presented to account for, or at least describe, the response of the public sector to cost-cutting campaigns by government. The first of these, which I shall call *Public Sector Generalisation No. 1*, states that: 'In general, the cost of the public sector of the economy cannot be cut by the action of government.' This hypothesis, proposed as a general, rather than a universal, rule, tells us that despite the nominal control of government, the costs of the public sector are in reality beyond the range of events whose outcomes can be determined by a democratic administration.

This appears to fly in the face of all reason. Since public sector events are supposed to represent the decisions of government, how can it seriously be proposed that the costs cannot be reduced by government? The answer is that there are forces which sustain public sector costs, forces which have their origins in the motivations and the behaviour of those concerned in public sector processes. What is being suggested by the proposed generalisation is that in most circumstances, these forces are greater than the forces which come from government aimed at a reduction in costs.[9]

Again, it might seem at first glance that the government need only make a decision and deploy its power accordingly. If it has failed thus far, it must be due to lack of resolution, lack of staying power, or some other cause of an unnecessary restraint. This view makes assumptions concerning the powers of government which may not be warranted in reality. Governments are not all-powerful; there are factors which they cannot control. The argument here comes down to the question of whether the forces which sustain public sector costs are among those factors.

There are physical realities, such as winter, for example, which the government cannot legislate away. Similarly there are aspects of human motivation and behaviour leading to economic realities which cannot be legislated away. Governments have tried for more than 4,000 years to control wages and prices by public decree. The record of success for those 4,000 years is entirely consistent. It is a story of universal failure. Temporary dams constructed by legislation in the stream of wage and price determination have always been swept away by a torrent of reality.

The claim asserted by *Public Sector Generalisation No. 1* is that the costs of the public economy have an upward pressure deriving from realities similar to those which determine wages and prices, and are just as incapable of being held down. Nothing is said in the generalisation about *increasing* the cost of the public sector: this may lie within the capacity of governments to achieve. All that is asserted is that governments cannot, in general, cut that cost. Nor is the generalisation proposed as a universal rule. There may be circumstances from time to time which can lead to lower the cost of the public sector: but it would be committing the fallacy of accident to suppose that they can generally be cut by government just because freak and unusual circumstances might allow it occasionally.

What is being proposed is that in the absence of these freak and unusual circumstances, in the normal run of behaviour of democratic governments, attempts by these governments to cut the costs of the state section of the economy will not be successful.

The second hypothesis, *Public Sector Generalisation No. 2*, is posited as a lemma to the first. It states that: 'Any apparent success by government in reducing the costs of the public sector of the economy is an illusion brought about by depletion of the capital stock, and will show an increase in the proportion of spending on the current side.' This hypothesis deals with those circumstances, unusual in themselves, in which the total spending figure for the public sector declines under the impact of government action. The hypothesis proposes that, in general, the apparent reduction will have been achieved at the expense of capital rather than current projects, and will reflect the fact that new capital projects have been abandoned or postponed, and renewal of existing stock is not keeping pace with the rate at which it is being used up.

The *Public Sector Generalisation No. 2* tells us that apparent cuts in public sector costs have not been achieved by the termination of programmes, nor by administrative or manpower economies in programmes which are retained. The cuts are achieved instead at the expense of new or renewal capital projects.

The net effect of the two generalisations leads to an even more surprising third hypothesis. Since the 'fat', or operating costs, cannot be cut by government action, and since any apparent cut is at the expense of capital stock, a *Public Sector Generalisation No. 3* can be advanced to state that: 'Government economy campaigns have the effect of lowering the productivity and efficiency of the public sector.' The reasoning is straightforward. If manpower and administrative costs are immune to cutting, and if the only apparent savings come at the expense of capital, the public sector after a campaign of cost-cutting operates on a lower level of capitalisation, but with no reduction in manpower. The 'wastage' of overhead cost remains as high, but is set against a lower base of capital stock. This can only mean a lowered efficiency. Moreover, with the deferment of capital projects, the output of public sector goods and services in the future will be lower, albeit without any proportional reduction in the manpower or administration levels.

One might suppose, after encountering the three public sector generalisations, that it is better not even to attempt to cut the costs of the state sector of the economy. After all, if the only success will be apparent, and if even that will cause lower productivity and efficiency, perhaps it would be as well to leave things alone. This view derives from the mistaken assumption that it is the efficiency of the public sector which is at issue.

Politicians of all parties have occasionally promised to secure us better value for money from public sector operations, while well-meaning retired civil servants have shown how inefficiency is rampant within their former profession and could be positively controlled by drastic action. They all rather miss the point. It is not the inefficiency of the public sector which causes the problem, but its existence and its size. The public sector itself is the evil, not any contingent qualities or properties which accompany its performance.

The public sector not only pre-empts the monies which could

otherwise be financing the expansion and development of business in response to real demand; not only does it take in taxation the purchasing power which might otherwise make effective the demand for the products and services of private business; it also involves the enforcement of collective choice to replace the free decisions of individuals in deciding priorities in life and allocating resources accordingly. It erodes, in other words, the part of our lives over which we exercise some power of decision and control.

The problem is not one of making the public sector more efficient; it is one of making it smaller. Even if a reduction in its costs is only temporary, and even if it comes at the expense of future capital projects, it does at least allow taxpayers to retain a fractionally greater amount of their resources to allocate individually. It may even be possible for circumstances to be contrived in which those future capital projects discarded from the public sector, will be taken up and completed by private business initiative.

The limits of privatisation

One solution to public sector costs has been proposed and found to have apparent advantages. If public programmes cannot either be curtailed or made cost-effective, perhaps they could instead be made private. If they were transferred across to the private sector of the economy, the reasoning runs, then most of the faults of collectivist economics would be eliminated.

A drawback to this proposed approach lies in the fact that many of the forces which resist cost-cutting operations within the public sector are equally resistant to the wholesale movement of those operations outside to the domain of private economics. It is politically unrealistic to expect that state education can be made private overnight, or the National Health Service abolished, however strong the criticisms levelled at them may be. For all its failings, the forces which sustain the NHS in place are far stronger than any political will to dislodge it.

Similarly in education, the voucher scheme has been known about for at least half a century, yet nothing has been done to implement it no matter what the shade of government in office. This is not due to any inherent fault in the economics of education vouchers, but to a political fault. The problem of giving education vouchers equal to the cost of a year's education per child is that it would involve an overnight revolution. All schools would become privately financed via vouchers, and would effectively become autonomous, rather than local authority controlled.

While bold members of a government might contemplate such a revolution, it is highly unlikely that any government could undertake it. Opposition from the teachers and the local authorities would be added to that from the administrators, locally and nationally, and orchestrated groups of parents who gain more from the present system. Very soon the level of media hostility would make the government uncertain of its own majority on the issue. As with the NHS, the forces in favour of the status quo would prevail.

The perception of the problem — demand-view economics

The problem is perceived in these terms: Since the cost of the public sector cannot be cut, and any attempted saving will make the situation worse by eating into capital stock and lowering productivity, the public sector operations must be transferred somehow into the private sector. Couched in those terms, it is easy to see why solutions have not been forthcoming, and why government ministers have found it easier to deride 'armchair' advocates of denationalisation than to denationalise.

The perception is erroneous. In the first place the cost-cutting efforts do not make things worse. Even if the public sector capital is depleted, a vacuum is created which can later be filled privately. The very necessity of future replacement of that capital will provide opportunities for private enterprise. The problem is not one of transferring public operations, complete with their capital, workforce, administration, working practices, history and traditions into the private sector. That would, indeed, be difficult, even if it were worthwhile. The problem is to have the goods and services presently produced in the public sector to be produced privately instead.

The false perception of the problem is brought about by looking at it in macroeconomic scale on the supply side of the equation. How can public sector supply be transferred to the private sector? It is the wrong question. A more valid question is this: *How can individuals who at present consume public sector goods and services be encouraged to demand private equivalents instead*?

The problem is not one of transferring production resources into the private sector, but of growing or developing a demand for private sector goods and services which will stimulate a supply response there. In other words, looking at the problem in microeconomic scale from the demand point of view, the problem is seen as one of making effective a demand which will result in the generating of new supply in the private sector, rather than in tackling the difficulty of transferring production resources.

Under this approach, there is no transfer of capital stock, of workforce, of administration, much less of working practices, history and traditions. The public sector supply is left in place. Attempts are made to cut its costs, but in the knowledge that expectations of success must be low. The focus of attention shifts instead to the demand view, to encouraging people of their own free will to seek alternative, private supply.

The aim is to ensure that growth takes place selectively in the private sector, thus diminishing the importance of the public supply as a proportion of total economic activity. To take away the demand for public sector goods and services is to remove one of the most powerful forces which work to sustain it. To create a growing number of persons whose demand is satisfied by a private sector supply is to create a force prepared to defend the means of their new satisfaction.

Promoting the demand

To a great extent the public sector supply is itself the most powerful incentive pushing people towards private consumption. With tax-supported expenditure determined more by political considerations than by consumer demand, and with a standing tendency to have the supply geared to meet the needs of the producers instead of the public which it nominally serves, the public sector is often characterised by queues, by inadequate and shoddy service, and by the absence of any opportunity for the expression of consumer choice. People turn, if they can, to a private sector alternative.

Secondly, the policy of requiring public sector economies will itself accelerate the move to private sector supply. The cost-cutting succeeds, if at all, in depleting the public capital, while maintaining or increasing current expenditure. The effect is to ensure that the future public sector will be under-capitalised, making it even less adequate. More and more, those who want a speedy and efficient service which is up to date with modern technology, and has some chance of meeting their requirements, will turn to private alternatives. The private sector provides a means whereby the queues can be escaped, along with the dreary conformity to minimum standards of basic utility which must characterise a service starved of capital to develop.

The one big obstacle to the development of private alternatives to public sector supply is the fact of compulsory payment for public services, whether consumed or no. Most people could pay for most medical insurance, or for the education of their children. Indeed, they do pay at present, and expensively, through the state system.[10] What many cannot do is to pay twice over. Having to pay taxes for a costly and inadequate state service, they have insufficient resources remaining to pay for a private service as well. The cost of exit from the public sector is high: it is the whole price of the alternative service.

An administration set on controlling the public sector by promoting the demand for private equivalents has the option of lowering the cost of exit from the public sector. If those who sought private supply were remitted some of what they had paid in taxation for the public supply, then many more would be able to pursue the option. At every price level there are those who cannot quite afford to buy: thus even modest tax rebates would tip some of those unable to afford alternatives at present into the ranks of those who could go it alone.

There are cases in which tax rebates offered to those who opt to buy private supply could yield a net gain to public funds. As each person decides to purchase a private alternative to the 'free' public service, a marginal saving is made possible by not having to provide the service for that person. As the percentage of those who opt out starts to mount up, so does the proportion of that potential marginal saving which can be achieved. While it is possible to suggest that the country would have to spend exactly the same on the NHS, even if less than half the population remained in it, this is unlikely to be true.

Careful market research can indicate the numbers likely to opt for private supply at various levels of tax rebate. The rebate offered by government can then be set so as to maximise the saving to public funds made possible by the numbers opting out. The effect of this would be to increase the spending per head to those who remained within the public service, a powerful argument to deploy against claims that the policy would make things worse for the poor.

There is a very good case for setting up a direct transfer system for the funding of state services, in such a way that for every person who opted out and accepted the rebate, that same sum would be deducted from next year's allocation for the department concerned. Such a system would kill two very dangerous birds. Firstly, it would make it less likely that departments would continue to claim increased budget allocations, even though the numbers served were declining. Secondly, it would defuse possible hostility from the Treasury on the ground that the rebates were revenues actually forgone, but the savings were purely hypothetical. To the Treasury, as to the Public Sector Borrowing Requirement, the rebates would be neutral. Less money taken in taxes would be balanced immediately by lower allocations to the departments concerned.

There is one final advantage to the policy of promoting demand for private alternatives to public supply. It is that it is a policy which would augment a trend already present. Instead of offering the prospect of an overnight revolution in the provision of service, the demand-view policy simply speeds up something that is already happening. If ever-increasing numbers struggle to afford the private alternative, even though they have to pay twice in full, and if opinion polls all show a huge desire to emulate this behaviour on the part of those who cannot yet afford to do so, it would appear that a policy of encouraging that demand would increase the pace of change, and meet with the support of those helped into the new alternative.

The advantage gained is that of a beneficiary class determined to sustain its new advantage of choice and high quality of service. It is a determination which can add force to the political will unable to attempt the task unaided.

The source and provision of the new private supply generated in response to the new demand is fortunately no concern of government. If the demand is promoted, the supply will be forthcoming to meet it in all kinds of unanticipated ways. Private initiative leaps to fill the vacuum of an unsatisfied effective demand: it is the government's task to pursue the policies which will create that vacuum.

The new private supply, from whatever source it arrives, creates with its investment and its manpower a new force to set against that from the manpower of the state system. If individuals gain the chance of better employment, more modern equipment, and the chance for higher pay and status from private firms opening up in the field, so much the less is their opposition to the process which brings this about.

The policy of controlling the public sector from the flanks, by promoting demand for private equivalents and alternatives, thus sets in motion real forces on the production as well as the consumption side, forces which bring its success within the realm of the politically possible. Under it there emerges the real possibility of a public sector held steady, or diminishing a little, while a vigorous private sector grows around it, reducing its importance as a proportion of total economic activity. To the scarcity of capital which the cost-cutting brings about, it adds a paucity of demand.

Controlling the costs of public sector supply is not something to be discouraged. But governments which undertake it should do so aware of the very modest results which can be expected at best. Instead of sinking into mutual recriminations about who was not tough enough, whose will failed first, and why everything was not done bigger and sooner, it might be as well if they understood the forces against them. An attempt to set in motion counter forces by encouraging the free decisions of millions of individuals, and helping to make possible what they already want to do, might merit some consideration as a useful supplement to the attempt.

FOOTNOTES

1. See the case of Leslie Chapman, a senior civil servant who attempted, with some degree of success, to cut the bureaucratic waste in his own departments. When brought in by London Transport his efforts were totally stymied by the resident bureaucrats, see Chapman, *Your Disobedient Servant*, Penguin, Harmondsworth, Middlesex, 2nd edn, 1979.

2. The realisation of this fact has been a major intellectual breakthrough of the past two decades. The false consciousness of 'political man', the idea that governmental, administrative and bureaucratic activities are immune from the same motivations — and the same sort of analysis — as the economic realm has been thoroughly shattered. See, for two useful introductions, Gordon Tullock, *The Vote Motive*, Institute of Economic Affairs, London, 1976; James M. Buchanan et al, *The Economics of Politics*, I.E.A., London, 1978. See also William A. Niskanan, *Bureaucracy and Representative Governnent*, Aldine, Atherton, New York, 1971; *Idem*, *Bureaucracy: Servant or Master?*, I.E.A., London, 1973; Gordon Tullock, *The Politics of Bureaucracy*, Public Affairs Press, Washington, D.C., 1965; Anthony Downs, *An Economic Theory of Democracy*, Harper and Row, New York, 1957; *Idem*, *Inside Bureaucracy*, Little, Brown, and Co.,

Boston, 1967; D. C. Mueller, 'Public Choice: A Survey', *Journal of Economic Literature*, Vol. 14, No. 2, June 1974; *Idem*, *Public Choice*, Cambridge University Press, 1979; R. D. Auster and M. Silver, *The State as Firm: Economic Forces in Political Development*, Martinus Nihoff, The Hague, 1979; D. K. Whynes and R. A. Bowles, *The Economic Theory of the State*, Martin Robertson, Oxford, 1980; Alan Peacock, *The Economic Analysis of Government and Related Themes*, Martin Robertson, Oxford, 1979; R. D. Leiter and G. Sirkin, eds, *Economics of Public Choice*, Cyrco Press, New York, 1975; J. T. Bennett, 'The Political Economy of Federal Government Paperwork', *Policy Review*, No. 7, Heritage Foundation, Winter 1979; James M. Buchanan and Richard D. Tollison, eds., *The Theory of Public Choice: Political Applications of Economics*, University of Michigan Press, Ann Arbor, 1972; A. Breton, *The Economic Theory of Representative Government*, Aldine Publishing, Chicago, 1974; *The Journal of Law and Economics*, Vol. XVIII, No. 3, December 1975, special issue on 'Economic Analysis of Political Behaviour'.

3. Although this argument can be found in various socialist polemics, it is hard to locate an academically respectable example. Perhaps the closest approximation can be found in R. Hemming and J. A. Kay, 'The Laffer Curve', *Fiscal Studies*, March 1980, although they are discussing tax take rather than marginal rates. They say 'It is possible that this process could go on indefinitely: as taxes rise higher and higher, the amount of work increases more and more as taxpayers struggle desperately to obtain sufficient income to live on. The limits of tax revenue are then set only by the limits of human endurance. . . . It is when people prefer to give up their leisure than their consumption when the tax burden increases that tax revenue may go on increasing indefinitely. For the majority of the studies cited, this is in fact the case. . . . The evidence runs strongly against the argument that tax rates in Britain, or any other country, are at levels such that the maximum available tax revenue is close to being obtained.'

4. Most of the standard texts on the subject are generally sceptical as to whether the 'price' effect (i.e. the incentive effect measured by the change in the cost of leisure) is sufficient to offset the income effect. Thus, see Alan Williams, *Public Finance and Budgetary Policy*, and John Due, *Government Finance*. In Britain, Barry Bracewell-Milnes has done a great deal of work in attempting to document and explicate this sceptical view. 'The Economics of Tax Reduction', in V. Tanzi, et al, *Taxation: A Radical Approach*, Institute of Economic Affairs, London, 1970, contains a Laffer-Curve type analysis. The Appendix, 'Maximum Tax Yield' in *The Camel's Back: An International Comparison of Tax Burdens*, Centre for Policy Studies, London, 1976, analyses the *relative* probabilities that different rates of tax are beyond the point of maximum revenue. *Self-Financing*

Reductions in Capital Taxes, Salisbury Group, London, 1981, extends the argument to *absolute* probabilities by distributing the negative incentive between tax rates. This latter point is explored in a more technical manner in Appendix V of *The Taxation of Industry*, Panopticum Press, London, 1982, wherein it is argued that the maximum-revenue yield of tax is not likely to be more than about 58% for any tax, except on possibly-addictive commodities like spirits and tobacco. For an American discussion of these issues see Arthur M. Oku, *Equality and Efficiency: The Big Trade Off*, Brookings Institute, Washington, D.C., 1975, pp. 96–98. A brief view on the generally detrimental effects of high taxation can be found in Bruce Bartlett, 'The Economics of Progressive Taxation', *Modern Age*, Vol. 22, No. 3, Summer 1978.

5. On the USA position, see R. David Ranson, 'Toward a Broader Picture of the Budget Deficit', *Policy Review*, No. 3, Winter 1978. On the failure of efforts by the Reagan team in the USA see David Boaz, 'The Budget: Snipping at the Status Quo', *Libertarian Review*, Vol. 10, No. 5, May 1981, and *Idem*, 'How to Really Cut the Budget', *Policy Report* (Cato Institute), Vol. 111, No. 5, May 1981.

6. And indeed, almost certainly are. See Digby Anderson et al, *Breaking the Spell of the Welfare State*, the Social Affairs Unit, London, 1981; *Idem*, *The Ignorance of Social Intervention*, Croom Helm, London, 1980; Colin Brewer and June Lait, *Can Social Work Survive?*, Maurice Temple Smith, London, 1980; C. Brewer et al, *Criminal Welfare on Trial*, Social Affairs Unit, London, 1981; June Lait, 'Central Government's Ineptitude in Monitoring Local Welfare', in A. Seldon, ed., *Town Hall Power or Whitehall Pawn*, op. cit.

7. See C. K. Rowley, 'Producer Pressure and Government Failure', *Journal of Economic Affairs*, Vol. 1, No. 1, October 1980. See also R. E. Wagner, 'Room and Bust: The Political Economy of Economic Disorder', *The Journal of Libertarian Studies*, Vol. IV, No. 1, Winter 1980; W. C. Mitchell, *The Anatomy of Public Failure: A Public Choice Perspective*, International Institute for Economic Research, Los Angeles, 1978; A. H. Meltzer, *Why Government Grows*, International Institute for Economic Research, Los Angeles, 1976.

8. Indeed, often quite irresponsibly so. See for example in Britain, the state's failure to maintain adequately many of the nation's sewer systems; the tardiness shown in the construction of the London flood barrier; the failure to expand or build more prisons.

9. See P. H. Aranson and P. C. Ordeshook, *The Political Bases of Public Sector Growth in a Representative Democracy*, Law and Economics Centre Working Paper, University of Miami School of Law, Coral Gates, Florida, 1978, and also their forthcoming book *The Failure of Representative Democracy*.

10. It is amazing how the myth that the Welfare State is actually redistributive in character maintains its predominance. In fact, the greater part of the welfare services received by individuals are paid for (in taxes of one form or another) by their recipients. This was pointed out by Anthony Fisher in his *Must History Repeat Itself?*, Churchill Press, London, 1974, pp. 81–85. A more recent and more thorough analysis of the statistics can be found in Arthur Seldon, *Charge*, Maurice Temple Smith, London, 1977, pp. 149–168. See also A. R. Prest, *Social Benefits and Tax Rates*, I.E.A., London, 1970. And see also, to the same effect, but from a socialist perspective, Julian Le Grand, *The Strategy of Equality*, Allen and Unwin, London, 1982. For American evidence on the realities of 'progressive' taxation, see Joseph Pechman, 'The Rich, the Poor and the Taxes they Pay', *The Public Interest*, No. 17, Fall 1969.

Small is rational

Let us inspect two types of approach to a problem which afflicts many advanced economies, the problem of urban congestion. We shall assume that a typical city — it could be Newcastle in England, or Washington in the USA — has developed in such a way that many of its citizens now live either in its outer periphery, or beyond its boundary altogether, and have to travel into work each morning and home again each evening.

The problem is that of too many vehicles. Although there are some suburban train services and a complex system of commuter bus routes serving the outer city, vast numbers come to work by car, with taxicabs supplying an insignificant proportion of the traffic. Traffic jams and congestion delays characterise the city every morning and evening at rush hour, and where access is limited, as at bridges and entry points onto major thoroughfares, the traffic can literally come to a standstill. Parking these vehicles within the city causes yet more problems, as their presence further restricts access down narrow streets.

There are many approaches to this problem, some of which would undoubtedly yield positive results. In the first place, one could simply prohibit private cars within the city, thus forcing traffic onto the public trains and buses. While this might have theoretical merits, the political resistance of city businesses and private citizens would effectively prevent its implementation. Still, it might be possible to achieve it in a limited area in the heart of the city, even though this would not solve the problem of commuter congestion.

A second, similar approach consists in making life difficult for the private car, without openly banning it. Private parking can be made prohibitively expensive, and so restricted that there are not enough spaces to cope with the demand. Certain key streets can be reserved for buses and taxis, forcing private cars into lengthy and difficult detours. Or lanes on busy roads may be set aside for exclusive use by public vehicles.

A third approach might be to embark on a major programme of road improvement, widening bottlenecks, constructing new expressways into the city, building bridges to take part of the traffic flow, and responding, in general, to the needs of the traffic. Many cities, to their cost, tried this approach. Its drawback is that it is expensive, and creates conditions which attract vehicles onto the roads. The congestion itself acts as a deterrent: ease it by new road construction and drivers not prepared to tolerate the old conditions will take advantage of the improvement. Thus traffic will once again expand until it becomes sufficiently congested to deter any more.

A fourth approach, often employed in bitter reaction to experience of the third, is a *laissez-faire* traffic policy. After the city has been carved up to make it fit for automobiles to live in, and congestion has built up again to the unacceptable level, city administrators might try doing nothing. It keeps congestion at its present level, instead of replacing houses with roads in order to achieve the same congestion with higher numbers. And it is cheaper.

All of these are methods of attacking the problem in one way or another, even the last one which attacks it with eyes firmly closed. There are two other types of solution, which have in common the fact that they do attempt to solve the problem, albeit in very different ways. They solve the problem in the sense that they give commuters a quick and relatively convenient journey into the city, and reduce the delays and costs which the traffic congestion has been causing. One method uses a large-scale solution, the other tackles it on the small scale.

The big solution involves the construction of a metro, or underground railway. Perceiving the problem as a lack of fast, cheap mass transit, the city authorities, usually with the help of funds from the national government, set about the construction of an underground network to link the city with its suburbs. Of course, the system is costly. With tunnels and track and stations to be built, it is a gigantic task taking many years to complete; but at the end of it there is a modern, cheap, fast service.

The first problem is cost. Cheap it might be to the user, but not to the payer. The fare prices have to be competitive with buses and cars, or the whole point of the system is lost. Underground railways are very, very expensive to build, and very expensive to run. They do not economise on fuel either in construction or in operation. For each passenger who purchases a ticket for his local metro, the local taxpayer or ratepayer might be paying as much again for that particular ride. When the costs of capital and interest are accounted, the local resident is paying many times the cost of the ticket.

Immediately after construction, a typical ride on the Bay Area Rapid Transit system (BART) of San Francisco cost the rider 72¢, and the local resident a further $3.76, or more than five times the fare. When the Washington metro opened, the taxpayer added $10.38 to each 40¢ or 55¢ paid by the passenger — twenty times the fare.

In addition to saddling the local taxpayer with huge costs stretching into the future, costs which must affect the viability of local businesses, the underground railway hits the local bus service. Although some private motorists are undoubtedly induced to leave the car at home, the metro's main pool of passengers is sucked from the local bus traffic, making the economics of those systems worse than it already is.

However, the system is at least modern. It looks large and impressive, and no doubt wins awards for its designers and builders. Local governments which build metro systems leave visible monuments to their efforts; they are seen to be doing things. The same cannot be said of the small-scale solution, the other method we inspect which actually tackles the problem.

The small solution is introduced from a standpoint which gives a different perception of the problem. The same facts are looked upon, but examined not in huge overall numbers which give rates of traffic flow and predictions of transfer to metro systems. Rather are they looked at from the point of view of the individual motorist who decides to bring his car into the city. Why does he reach that decision? The answer is probably couched in terms of convenience and price. He wants a method of transport which will take him from as near his home as possible to as near his place of work as can be managed. He wants as few changes, as little exposure to the elements, and as short a waiting time as can be achieved. He also wants a fast trip, a clean trip, a comfortable trip, and a cheap one.

Plainly the existing system does not satisfy the commuter. For all of the cost and the congestion he must go through, he prefers his own car to the public system which is available. When we start to ask why it is that the public sector supply is unsatisfactory, we start to receive helpful answers which point the way towards policy.

The typical public transport for most advanced cities is inflexible. Established and built up in an age when large numbers wished to travel along fixed routes, it has probably not kept pace with new circumstances which have given the city a more diffuse population.

Use of the public supply probably involves transport to the point from where it operates. If the car has to be used for that journey, it is more convenient to use it for the entire trip than to face the change and the wait.

The public supply is often uncomfortable and dirty. Old vehicles which have grown shabby are to be expected. As with other public sector goods and services, the capital has been run down because it is easier to save there than on the current account. The motorist prefers his new clean car to the old and filthy train. Furthermore, inadequate capital renewal means crowded conditions on public transport: the motorist prefers the comfort and space of his own vehicle.

The quality of service on the public system is probably not what the average commuter wants, either. The monopoly position, combined with the unlikelihood of a public sector employee losing his job through lack of custom, have created conditions under which the desires of the consumer are of little account. The interests of those engaged in the production of the service loom much larger in consideration when service quality is determined. Much is done for the convenience of the administration and the workforce which would never be accepted in any private service.

The reason why private companies have not sprung up to provide the transport service which customers require, is that they have not been allowed to. Legal prohibition has prevented the competition. Taxicabs, which might have undertaken the task of taking commuters onto the fixed route public system, have been too scarce and too expensive. This is because their numbers have been officially limited, and because licences and conditions of service have been issued in a way calculated to keep up the price. Private motorists have normally been forbidden to load their cars with paying neighbours, while minibuses have been banned on alleged safety grounds.

Once the problem has been perceived in these terms, from the point of view of the motivated decision of the individual commuter, all kinds of ways begin to suggest themselves of encouraging him to decide to leave the car at home. If unregulated bus services are permitted, smart businessmen will seize the opportunity to make good by providing a door-to-door service. If the 8–12-seater 'jitney' is allowed to ply along relatively predictable routes, but ready to go a few blocks out of its way for a marginally higher fare, thousands of them may soon be carrying full passenger loads.[1]

Relaxation of the prohibition on private drivers carrying passengers for fares will undoubtedly put many people together who travel presently in separate cars each. Enterprising businesses or the local authority might even run a computer 'matching' service to put them in touch with each other. The regulations which govern entry into cab-driving might be scrapped, as should limitation on numbers, as should rules which prevent efficient use. Cabs might be found at railway and bus termini, with blackboards indicating their destination, waiting to fill up with separate passengers on the style of the Israeli 'shiruts', or their equivalents throughout the Middle East.

All of the measures so far suggested as part of the small-scale solution involve the local authority not in doing new things, but in ceasing to do what it is already doing. They involve it in the removal of rules, regulations and restrictions. They are only the beginning. A government determined to apply the small-scale solution could encourage commuters to arrange for a door-to-door contract bus service, by arranging for the fares thus paid to be deductible from tax base, returning thereby some of the tax used to sustain the public transport. The prospect of each 48-seater bus replacing 48 private cars on the rush-hour roads might encourage the government to realise that it could save more than the tax concession would cost it.

There are innumerable measures which local and national governments could take to tip the balance of that decision by each motorist. A list could be gained immediately by seeing what goes on in other cities around the world. In a few, and only a few, the problem is being tackled the small way. The smallness is, alas, a political disadvantage. The solution does not look good. Certainly, it is very cheap; and certainly, it is very effective. But it does not provide gleaming buildings or other visible marks of an active and 'caring' local administration.

The small solution is not particularly 'modern', either. It will not win too many international prizes. It is, however, very flexible. It will meet changes in demand with immediate changes in supply. It will supply a range of variety and choice to meet individual needs and preferences. It will keep up to date with its equipment and techniques. Those who fail to do so will lose their trade to those who do. It will continue to innovate in comfort and service for the same reason. On top of all this can be added the fact that it is easy to administer, because it needs only to be left alone and watched, and that it does not involve local rate-payers or tax-payers in a huge burden of capital debt for its construction, or in a lifetime commitment to subsidising its operation.

Clearly, from an examination of the two approaches to the problem of urban congestion, many observers would opt for the one which the microeconomic approach suggests, rather than that whose origins lie in macroeconomic calculation. They see that the small-scale approach practically allows the problem to solve itself. It might be argued, though, that the example chosen is one uniquely suited to small-scale operation. Outside of transport, it could be claimed, there is less room for the little man.

The claim is not a valid one. At no stage did authority make a commitment to small size solutions; these were the ones forthcoming when individuals were motivated to respond. Some of the responses elicited by the actions may be large. Huge bus companies owning hundreds of vehicles and ferrying tens of thousands of passengers each day are by no means out of the question. The answer is small from the point of view of the customer. Given the right conditions, all kinds of solutions might be forthcoming.

The difference between the two approaches is not merely the difference between acting on the large or the small scale; it is also the difference between taking the standpoint of the producer or the consumer. The solution which took the large scale approached the problem from the point of view of supply: given a shortage of transport of a certain type, the answer was to produce more of it; and given that there was a vast shortage, the production must be large. The small-scale solution took the standpoint of the consumer. Instead of summing the different needs and desires of different individuals, and of aggregating their different responses, it attempted to create conditions under which, for each, a supply would be forthcoming. At no stage in the small solution does authority attempt to provide or assist the supply.

The actions are calculated instead to act on demand. By removing the restrictions and adding incentives, the demand is made effective. Instead of offering loans or providing vehicles, or assisting the production of transport services in any other way, the authorities give the best assistance they can by setting free the demand. Given that demand, supply will come in unanticipated and incalculable ways. By this approach the authorities eschew the task of large-scale provision of a fairly standard product for all, and permit the differing demands to be met in different ways.

Far from being suitable only for the field of transport, the same approach can be applied in most areas of public supply. By thinking small, that is, by perceiving the problem from the demand view, solutions can be engendered which are radically different from the traditional mass supply which has characterised public provision. It is possible, indeed likely, that the total volume of new transport service provided will be larger by adding together all of the bus, shirut and jitney places used each day, than it would be with a publicly funded metro system.

Similarly in other areas of mass supply, more provision might be gained by a combination of small-scale operations than by the large-scale public sector service which is the alternative. In some of these areas, such as in health and in education, so ingrained is the habit of thinking in terms of what supply can be afforded and how it might be stretched to cover shortages or extended to new fields, that the demands of individual consumers are often perceived as irrelevant, sometimes as an intruding nuisance. Administrators of education are quite firmly opposed to the idea of parents being allowed to shop around to choose the school they prefer; and teachers, while welcoming parental interest as a means of supporting their authority, are against parental 'interference' in the educational process.

The same syndrome is repeated everywhere. Any product or service which is perceived from the standpoint of supply will become producer-oriented. A large-scale supply, planned centrally, will produce more gain for those involved in the production of it than for those who are its nominal beneficiaries. Railways in Britain are nominally for the benefit of the travelling public and the firms who send goods across the country; coalmines are supposed to produce coal for the nation, that is, the people; the National Health Service is designed to take away the worries of health care; the education system is to provide every child with a free, high quality education. The list goes on.

In reality, the people employed in the railways, the mines, the NHS or in state education are the main beneficiaries. At both management and labour levels, the various services find the demands of the employees more pressing than those of the distant public. The administration and workforce put real and immediate pressure on the system, the consumers do not. The supply is not geared to what people express real demand for, indeed, it excludes any mechanism for determining such a thing. It is geared instead to supplying that which it is convenient to supply.

There are, thus, three specific criticisms to be levied at the large-scale, centrally-planned solution. It is very expensive, it is inflexible, allowing few opportunities for variety and choice, and it is not structured in a way which will enable it to recognise and meet demand. On each of these three points the small-scale solution has the advantage.

Analogues of the two approaches inspected to deal with the problem of urban congestion can be found in practically every area of the public sector. The mass supply on the large scale could be replaced by a series of small measures to make effective a demand which would yield a totally different kind of supply. A localised problem perceived as a shortage of school places could be tackled by the building of a 2,000-pupil all-in comprehensive school. Or it could be approached from the point of view of what the parents want, and of making effective their demands. If parents were to receive a tax rebate for not consuming the state school place to which their child was entitled, the different requirements and wants might be met in a variety of ways.

Some children might be sent to boarding schools, with the tax rebate contributing to fees which could not have been afforded otherwise. Some, undoubtedly, would go to specialist schools to develop natural talents in such areas as music or mathematics. Given the demand made effective by tax rebates, new, small schools would be created locally using converted houses. Consortia of teachers might establish their own, small schools. Groups of parents might start others, hiring teachers in accordance with their educational preferences. Church-related schools, charity-funded schools, experimental schools; the variety which might spring up is enormous.

From the point of view of supply, it makes little difference whether the money is used to build one giant all-purpose school, or whether it results in the same number of pupils receiving an education in a variety of different small schools of different types. It may be argued that there are economies of scale in the larger school, that there are expensive pieces of equipment, such as computers or scientific apparatus, which no school should be without, and yet which cannot be afforded by small schools catering for very few pupils. The same might be said of sports facilities.

What would happen in practice, were the small-scale solution to be implemented, would be the combination of smaller schools for the purchase and use of expensive equipment, or the establishment of common central facilities on an independent basis, with the small schools as customers. In any case, there are diseconomies of scale in the large school. The need for a purpose-built school commits a great deal of capital, whereas the smaller schools can be based in converted buildings. The large school has huge costs for heating and security, and must count vandalism and discipline as problems meriting much more time and attention than they require in the smaller school. Finally, one might add that there is difficulty at the big school in giving individual attention to each child, the attention which can make the difference to the child's motivation.

From the point of view of supply, that is, from the government's desire to have each child receiving an adequate education, there is little difference between the large solution and the small one. From the demand view, however, the difference is vast. It is the difference between a take-it-or-leave-it place in a standardised state school, with all that this entails, and a choice of several different types and sizes of schools with different specialisations in various locations. The small solution brings in the choice and variation which enables differing requirements to be met simultaneously.

Again, a similar problem could be presented in health. A perceived shortage of beds could be met by the building of a giant hospital with its open plan wards and its routines designed for efficient running. Or the funds could be returned via tax rebates to the individual, and used to purchase places in a number of small-scale private clinics. The same number of beds might be provided, but the difference to the consumer would be just as great as in transport or education. The flexibility of the small-scale solution allows individual preferences to be satisfied.

Private insurance provides the means of implementing the small, demand-oriented solution. Those who opt out of the public supply could have returned to them the funds the public sector will not now have to spend on them. The private insurance companies would be the intermediaries through which the now effective demand was expressed. It is quite possible that, similar to the forecast in education, the demand would be met by a collection of small private clinics, low in capital cost, reasonably cheap to run, and able to provide both the specialisations and the consideration for the individual which the larger hospitals find so difficult.

In each case where the problem is looked at from the demand view, there is the prospect of allowing a supply to be generated to solve the problem. In many cases it is the public supply and the compulsion to pay for it which *is* the problem. It pre-empts in taxation the funds which people could otherwise have used to obtain their own supply from independent sources. The fact that in the overwhelming bulk of cases those who seek an independent supply have to pay twice over leaves them with no choice but to accept the public product.

As was evident from inspection of the transport example, the public supply can be expected to have more than the disadvantages of large-scale supply, that is, costliness and inflexibility. It can also be expected to show the consequences of inadequate capitalisation, and of an organisation which makes more concessions to producers than to consumers. One expects the public service to be shoddy and inadequate. Not enough public investment has gone in to keep up its capitalisation. Its equipment will be worn and outmoded, and it will not normally be up to date in its techniques or service offerings. The propensity to serve the convenience of the producers will usually mean that it is difficult to obtain service at awkward times, or which differs in any way from the standardised output.

While one might suppose that a good injection of public cash would solve most of these problems, one would be mistaken to do so. The forces which determine the behaviour of the public sector remain in place. The same tendency to spend on the current at the expense of the capital side, the same propensity to place producer needs above those of consumers are still there. Any influx of public cash would show a distribution pattern much as before, with a large part of it going to increase the remuneration of the labour force, to enable even more restrictive working conditions and practices to be claimed, and to finance an even higher ratio of manpower to output. Administrators would find it even harder to resist wage demands than at present, and only a tiny proportion of the new influx would go towards new capital spending.

To pinpoint the failings of the public sector as deriving from inadequate finance is to miss the point. The reasons why the finance is inadequate have to be explored: if these turn out, as they do, to be problems of allocation of available cash, then it is no solution to pump in new supplies without tackling the forces which lead to the misallocation.

There are other problems concerned with the overall funding of the large-scale solution. While the institutional structure and immunity to consumer pressures distorts the allocation of available resources towards the producers, the political setting imposes serious limitations on the total spending level. The funding is determined more by the general economic health of the nation and by what governments feel are expedient levels of taxation and borrowing, than by the need to meet demand within specific areas. There is no way of knowing with certainty, for example, how much people in Britain would have been prepared to spend on health services if they had been permitted to buy what they wanted.[2]

There is a rough indication to be found in terms of what has been spent in other countries, and what has been spent in the minute private health sector in Britain. The indications are that it would have been larger than the taxation resources which governments have felt able to levy and commit. Most other countries spend a higher proportion of GNP on health than Britain does. This indicates the possibility at least that individuals left to express their own preferences and priorities might have chosen to allocate more to health care than they have been permitted to do so. This, in turn, suggests that people might demand a higher standard of care, as well as a more expensive one, than they have been receiving.

With the insensitivity which the large solution shows towards individual needs and wants, it is difficult to tell what public requirements are. Perceived from the supply viewpoint, doubtless some planners prevail over others in deciding which possible services should receive priority over others. The decisions are made, and an ambulance service is financed to provide 93% of its trips for non-emergency cases, effectively a state-funded taxi service to take people to and from treatment centres. Meanwhile, the decision is also taken as to the proportion of kidney patients whose lives we can afford to save.

These decisions may bear no relation at all to those which individuals would have opted for if permitted by law to do so, and if left with sufficient resources to make their demands effective. Individuals exert influence on the large solution only crudely and at great distance through the political process, and subject to all of the diffusion and signal scatter which this process involves. With solutions of the smaller scale in effect, people may well have chosen patterns of allocation which left them to make their own way to hospitals and clinics for non-emergency cases, but provided sufficient dialysis machines and transplant operations for cases of renal failure.

The large solution does not have that kind of information. It is on a scale where aggregation has lost the knowledge of individual differences and preferences, and where the information comes from the mind of the planners. The small solution retains the information at the individual level because it does not deal in the giant aggregates; and the information which it processes is far greater than that which any human mind could hold. In the small solution, the information is held in the system. Human motivation is triggered by opportunities presented. The relation of individual requirements to available supply is expressed by a price mechanism which prompts people to action, given their natures.

The small solution is more rational. It does not sacrifice more information in order to use less: it does not forgo detailed knowledge in order to substitute general estimates: it does not reject an exact measurement in order to replace it by a rough average. It does not, above all, seek to produce at great cost and effort a supply which corresponds only in vague and fuzzy outline to the reality which an effective demand would have called into being unaided.

There remains the argument that if authority were to give free rein to demand, rather than focussing on perceived supply needs, there would be those unable to bid in such a market. In the first place, they would be few in number. It is a long exploded fallacy that in public sector provision the rich pay for the poor. The rich do, indeed, pay more, but there are not enough of them to make a significant difference. The norm is that people pay for themselves, that what they receive back is roughly what they pay in various taxes, minus, of course, the cut which is absorbed in administration.[3]

Most people, therefore, would be better off. Paying their money for independent supply would probably command them more resources than they can achieve from the public sector. They would be buying from producers with more efficient labour, higher productivity, and more advanced technology. Furthermore, they would be buying from a market which catered to the variety of individual tastes and preferences. Most people would find themselves able to obtain an adequate supply for a price they could afford; and it would be a supply closer to their individual needs than the standardised public supply could achieve.

There would, however, be some who could not. Even after tax rebates and other concessions have been taken into account, there would still be those unable to afford what society deemed to be acceptable levels of health, education, etc. Society would have several options, but two present themselves immediately. Either they would remain dependent on the public supply, which would come increasingly to cater for those with no other option, or they could be funded to become effective consumers in a private market. Welfare payments or vouchers could take them into the ranks of those who could afford adequate service.[4]

To argue that either of these solutions would create two classes of provision is to close one's eyes to the fact that there is already such a division. In any allocation of scarce public resources, the articulate and self-confident middle classes are not left behind in claiming their share.[5] In any event, it is an arguable proposition that everyone should receive an inferior service in order to prevent different standards. True, some parents batter their children: only a few persons, however, would advocate that all children should be taken away from their parents in order to prevent those few cases. The normal solution would be to allow the most who can to take care of their own provision, and concentrate special treatment on the very small number who cannot.

It is certainly true that if most people were able to allocate their own resources to meeting their own individual needs and preferences, it would be easier to concentrate more public provision on those in real need. It would be easier still, however, to concentrate welfare provision into their hands to enable them to express their needs in the same way as did the vast majority.

There is, finally, the view that variety itself is wrong, and that people should not be permitted to express different preferences and needs at all. This view says that people should receive the same treatment despite their differences, and should receive identical health care, education, transport, etc. For that matter, the principle could be extended to include identical food, clothing, housing and consumer goods. The view is simply pernicious, reflecting a desire to have people live out the fantasies of the planners, instead of living their own lives. It is a view which treats people as sheep and planners as shepherds, and does not correspond either to reality, or to the domain of the morally acceptable.[6]

In the real world people are motivated differently. They act in a pursuit of values which include self-interest and the good of others, and they act from different perceptions and with different priorities. All too often they are catered for by the confiscation of their resources to fund the provision of an inadequate and inflexible public supply. It is possible, instead, to apply the small solution, to return them sufficient of their resources to make them able to command independent sources of supply, sources which will find all kinds of innovative and incalculable ways of satisfying that demand.

The small solution may not be particularly modern. It might be unexciting, and have few monuments of grandiose proportions to flatter the vanity of legislators. But it does have its merits. It provides the variety of services required to meet a variety of needs. It keeps up to date with advances in technology and service. It is both cheap and efficient: it is rational, and it works.

FOOTNOTES

1. For a very thorough examination of the whole question of the regulation of taxicabs, its disastrous consequences, and the viability of an unlicensed 'jitney' system, see the essay by Sandi Rosenbloom — a fellow of the Institute of Transportation and Traffic Engineering - 'Taxis and Jitneys: The Case for Deregulation', *Reason*, Vol. 3, No. 11, February 1972. Ms. Rosenbloom concludes, 'that for over 50 years and through two world wars there has been a series of transportation needs that are not met by fixed-route or fixed-rail large vehicle systems. . . . For over 50 years there have been people with enough initiative to be willing to provide services to fill these transportation demands and enough knowledge or common sense to know *where* the demand actually is. And just like clockwork, fixed-route operators, themselves unable or unwilling to provide the demanded services, have managed to protect their interests against competition by restricting the flexible service out of business. . . .', p. 12.

2. But see the attempts by the Institute of Economic Affairs to make some sort of assessment, using opinion polls, of the public's desire for choice in the purchase of further 'social services'. The Institute held its 'Choice in Welfare' surveys in 1963, 1965, 1970 and 1978. For a detailed account of these surveys and their significance see Ralph Harris and Arthur Seldon, *Over-Ruled on Welfare: The Increasing Desire for Choice in Edu-*

cation and Medicine and its Frustration by 'Representative' Government, I.E.A., London, 1979.

3. See the evidence cited in footnote 8 of Chapter 2.

4. The idea of the use of the 'voucher' to help the poor, instead of direct and centralised state provision of the services themselves, has long been a feature of liberal ideology, from Tom Paine — in *The Rights of Man* in 1792 — to Milton Friedman in *Free to Choose*. On the voucher idea in general, and particular applications, see M. & R. Friedman, *Free to Choose*, Secker and Warburg, London, 1980, pp. 158–188; A. F. Ott, *Education Through Choice*, Institute for Economic Studies, Worcs., Massachusetts, 1980; R. G. Scott et al, *The Educational Voucher System*, National Council for Educational Standards, Esher, 1980; A. C. F. Beales et al, *Education: A Framework for Choice*, I.E.A., London, 2nd edn, 1970; A. T. Peacock and J. Wiseman, *Education for Democrats*, I.E.A., London, 1970; E. C. West, *Economics, Education and the Politicians*, I.E.A., London, 1968; A. Maynard, *Experiment With Choice In Education*, I.E.A., London, 1975; E. B. Edwards, *Education Vouchers For Blacks and Hispanics*, Citizens For Educational Freedom, Washington, D.C., 1976. However see George H. Pearson, 'The Case Against Education Vouchers', *Reason*, Vol. 3, No. 1/2, April/May 1971, for a libertarian criticism of the concept, whether as an aim in itself or as a transitional measure to a completely free society.

5. Many scholars, of diverse political views, are at last beginning to recognise that state monopoly provision of services does not guarantee equality of treatment within them — indeed, that articulate and assertive middle and upper class individuals profit within such systems and lower class individuals are disadvantaged in ways which would not occur within a free market system. A. H. Birch, 'Economic Models in Political Science: The Case of Exit, Voice and Loyalty', *British Journal of Political Science*, January 1975, discusses this and provides some concrete examples from the author's own experiences (see pp. 77–79). Professor Brian Barry's *Sociologists, Economists and Democracy*, Collier-Macmillan, N.Y., 1970, uses economic tools and the concepts of 'exit, voice and loyalty' to explain why this is the case. Also, see his 'Exit, Voice and Loyalty', *British Journal of Political Science*, Vol. IV, 1974. The liberal and libertarian view that *in reality* the 'poor' and disadvantaged gain nothing by the welfarist and statist legislation passed allegedly in their interest is buttressed by a wider stream of economic and social analysis. Thus, such Chicago School economists as George J. Stigler ('The Theory of Economic Regulation', *Bell Journal of Economics and Management Science*, No. 2, Spring 1971), have shown that interventionist measures, in spite of their altruistic and humanitarian rhetoric, generally originate in a special interest group seeking privilege, and are almost certainly dominated and used by such interests

whenever instituted. Similarly, a long but relatively neglected stream of liberal class analysis has demystified the realities of interventionism and statism. On the latter see Chris R. Tame, 'Against The New Mercantilism: The Relevance of Adam Smith', *Il Politico*, Vol. XLIII, No. 4, and *Idem*, 'Introduction to Libertarian Class Analysis', a paper delivered to the Centre For Policy Studies, 1978.

6. For some libertarian views on the issue of equality see H. George Resch, 'Individuality, Equality and Compulsory Schooling', Conference on Compulsory Education, Centre For Independent Education/Institute For Humane Studies, Milwaukee, Wisconsin, November 1972; H. Schoeck, 'Individuality vs. Equality', in F. Morley, ed., *Essays on Individuality*, University of Pennsylvania Press, Philadelphia, 1958; George Harris, *Inequality and Progress* (1897), Arno Press, New York, 1972; Ludwig Von Mises, 'Equality', pp. 27–30, in *Idem*, *Liberalism: A Socio-Economic Exposition* (1962), Sheed, Andrews and McMeel, Kansas City, 1978; Murray N. Rothbard, *Power and the Market: Government and the Economy*, Institute For Humane Studies, Menlo Park, California, 1970, pp. 157–160; Anthony Flew, *The Politics of Procrustes: Contradictions of Enforced Equality*, Maurice Temple Smith, London, 1981.

Economics as a creative process

Economic activity is inherently unpredictable for a variety of reasons. Its outcomes have their ultimate origins rooted in human action; it is the decisions of individuals to allocate or withhold resources which finally determine economic events. Although we can look at past occurrences and draw up impressive tables of empirical evidence on the factors which influence those decisions, we cannot inspect the processes which determine them. New circumstances may lead to people making different decisions to the ones they made before.[1]

Our empirical evidence is about the past. It can only guide us to the future if we use it to propose and test relationships which claim to fit future application as well as historical evidence. In fields which concern themselves with human behaviour, however, we do not find the regularities which characterise the world of science. Free will, individuality, the lack of objective observation, and the possibility of events being influenced by the predictions themselves, all conspire to leave us in the human studies with little more than a few generalisations about human nature.[2]

By dealing with very large numbers and processing statistical information, we might be able to project a few pattern generalisations to give us the rough shape of events, if not the detail, but even here we gain no more than broad probabilities which admit of counter-examples. People act purposefully, unlike stones and billiard balls, and they may purposefully decide to do other than was predicted for them.[3]

The future state of society cannot be predicted because it depends, among other things, on the knowledge that is available to it. To predict the future state, we would have to predict what that knowledge would be: but to know it now would make it present knowledge.[4] Similar reasoning leads us to be similarly pessimistic about our chances of successfully predicting a future economic state. Economic performance depends upon economic and technological innovation. Since we cannot anticipate future innovation, we cannot claim accuracy for our economic predictions.

There is a close parallel between economic activity and the acquisition of knowledge; and an important role in each for creativity, something which not only eludes any attempt to predict it, but which regularly falsifies the predictions we have made in other fields. The two activities parallel each other because both are examples of our attempts to achieve our purposes. We try to predict the observed world so we can control our circumstances, and we engage in economic activity to allocate our resources according to our priorities, and to maximise the advantage which accrues to us. Both of them involve the attempt to increase the extent to which our own hands can shape our futures.

The methods we employ in each activity show similarities, too. To increase our knowledge we test theories competitively to see which ones best serve our purposes. We discard those which have lower predictive power in favour of the more successful ones. The theories we reject have not been 'proved wrong', for this is as impossible as proving them right. They have been shown to be less successful than their rivals at enabling us to predict things. There is a very important sense in which theories are not right or wrong at all, but are the best inventions which our minds can produce to help us predict what we shall observe. The terminology which speaks of the 'discovery' of knowledge, especially scientific knowledge, is a misleading one. We do not 'discover' knowledge which is already there, we create it. Scientific theories are invented by us for our purposes, and it would be more accurate to describe Newton as the *creator* of the theory of gravity than as the man who discovered it.[5]

The distinction is important because it pinpoints the importance of the creative process in making progress towards human goals. Newton invented in his mind a model universe in which a gravitational force functioned according to an inverse square law. This invention enabled him and us to predict what we observe more effectively than had previous inventions.

In economic activity, too, we make attempts to achieve goals, and reject the less successful in favour of the more so. We modify our attempts in the light of our experience with them. We make guesses about what to do, not random, mindless guesses, any more than we make in science, but inspired guesses which use our creativity and intelligence. We test them and retain the ones which serve us best. The man who devises a new product or process, an innovation in technique or in marketing, is being as inventive as the scientist who devises a theory. Both of the inventions will stand or fall by their ability to out-perform their rivals.

It is apparent already that the similarities derive from the fact that each is a specific case of the more general evolutionary method of change. An innovation introduced into the status quo is found superior under test, and survives at the expense of its rivals. For science, economics and other human activities it is of crucial significance that the innovations are introduced by the creative mind of man, rather than, like biological mutations, from the blind workings of a random chance.

Of course the majority of people, in either economic activity or the acquisition of knowledge, may prefer not to make these bold leaps into the unknown. For most people, the conjectures they make may be small ones, well within the accepted and established behaviour range of their fellows. While a few truly inventive and adventurous minds might leap into the far unknown, the rest might feel more comfortable keeping company with the multitude and following at a safe distance. Just as most scientists spend their time polishing the edges of the larger theories instead of seeking to replace them, so do most people in economic life make their decisions within the range of what others have made available, rather than seeking to introduce a dramatic new reality.

The new economic realities do arrive, just as do the new theories of science, and they have the effect of changing the entire paradigm within which people live and work. They can be just as upsetting and unsettling to those who prefer the comfort of established behaviour patterns, even as they expand the opportunities available to us. Entrepreneurial activity takes place at many levels of innovation, from the trader who spots an opportunity to maximise his returns by altering a price, to the person who introduces a major technological advance into an established market. The guess of the entrepreneur, his creative act, is like the mutation in biology. If it outperforms its rivals, it survives and brings a new reality; if it fails it disappears.[6]

The products of the creative imagination are as unpredictable in economic life as they are in scientific research; and each can no more be foreseen than can the mutations which emerge in the biological process. All of them, in their way, contrive a new and unknown reality.

The process by which change is effected in the economic sphere may be inspected by following a fairly typical example. We might watch an entrepreneur who has calculated that, by dealing in very large volumes, he can accept lower profit margins per item, and present a lower price to the customer. Having made arrangements to ensure sufficient sales outlets, and to advertise the new low prices he is offering, he presents the public with the option of buying from him at a lower price. All other things, such as quality and convenience, being taken into account, if sufficient numbers switch their custom to him, his gamble is justified.

Rival dealers now have the option of accepting a much reduced share of the market, or trying to match his initiative. They, too, can consider lowering the price and trying to make up in volume what they forgo in profit per item. Some will perhaps leave the particular line of business, yielding the field to the innovative interloper. Others will adjust to the new reality, maybe between them turning what was a luxury trade into a mass market.

In the process of this, the public has gained the advantage of the low prices. Some can buy who could not previously afford it, while others have more resources to allocate elsewhere. A new reality has been established by the creative act of an individual seeking to improve his own position. This is a fair account, in outline, of what happened in the field of international air transport. A high-priced luxury trade catering primarily to the business traveller turned within a decade into a mass market characterised by ferocious price competition. In the industry concerned there were cartels and government regulations to be overcome along the way, but the new reality was that most people found transatlantic travel within their price range. Gentlemanly and regulated competition in the quality of in-flight catering gave way to discount and stand-by fares. The entrepreneurs left their mark; and even though one of the pioneers was a casualty, the mass market remained.

One obvious and important difference between innovations in economics and the mutations which lead to biological change is that the ideas of economics can be copied.[7] The mutation can only be imparted to offspring, but the economic innovation can be taken up by competitors. And while an unsuccessful mutation leads to the death of its bearer, an entrepreneur can survive several failures, even bankruptcies, to come back with a winner.

It is because of the way in which we can transfer ideas that our progress in intellectual life takes place at a much faster rate than our biological development. Evolution has made negligible changes to the human race over the same period which has witnessed a total transformation of its economic status. Innovation in biology benefits only the bearer and its successors; creativity in human activities can benefit everyone.

An important feature of economic change emerges from the inspection of its processes. It is that economic progress is not achieved by any logical development of existing circumstances, but as the result of a creative leap beyond those circumstances. Economic development may appear to derive from a planned extension of the status quo, just as scientific advances may appear to come from an inductive extension of present knowledge. The appearance is in each case illusory. The advance is achieved by testing against the status quo an innovation which leaps beyond it. If the innovation is found preferable to its rivals, it survives as part of a new reality.

Creativity is thus an essential component of economic progress; no development can take place without it, and yet no plan can produce it, measured and metered, to a predetermined timetable. Creativity comes from individuals, not from planners, and stands as guarantor for the falsification of all planned economic development. As it produced the package holiday, so it produced the ballpoint pen, the hyper-market, the personal computer and the electronic toy, all of which made nonsense of economic plans and forecasts.

Though unable to predict what innovations will be thought of and introduced, we are able to contrive circumstances in which creativity will be allowed to play its part in promoting economic advances. It is exercised in response to opportunity; people innovate because they stand to gain by doing so. Perceiving or anticipating a demand, the innovator sees a chance to achieve personal advantage by meeting it. If his new product or process or method of organisation or service leads people to satisfy that demand by freely turning to his supply, then he gains the economic benefits.

Economic progress and development can be encouraged, if not planned, by maximising the opportunities for creative innovation. Since it is produced to serve a perceived or anticipated demand, it has most play in those sectors of the economy which are demand-oriented. The production of a public sector supply takes place, for the most part, within an established economic paradigm. The quality and quantity are planned in accordance with what is available, and the problems are those of allocating resources and labour such that production does indeed take place according to the predetermined schedule.

The public supply, furthermore, prevents people from transferring their custom to any more attractive innovation which might be produced. Not only does it enforce payment by taxation, but it usually prevents by monopoly legislation the introduction of alternatives. There may be a few encouragements for innovation, by means of various special remuneration schemes, but these pale into insignificance compared to the incentives which a demand-led area of the economy offers naturally.

In general it is the private, rather than the public economy which is characterised by creative progress. Public sector goods and services tend to lag. If a public supply is protected by monopoly, even innovations borrowed from abroad or adapted from the private sector will tend to be introduced much more slowly than they would in a demand-led sector. Given public capital in being, and the commitment to established methods, there is no need to have innovations introduced at a disruptive rate. The monopoly prevents people taking their custom elsewhere; they have to be content with what they are given. It is more convenient to introduce any changes only when existing capital stands in need of replacement anyway.

It was public sector monopoly supply which kept the British telephone service in a technological backwater, even while all kinds of advances were being made in response to the demands of consumers in countries where this was permitted. The sudden influx into Britain of push-button dialling, memory telephones, automatic redial, cordless telephones and a range of design choices for hand-sets was not caused by any sudden surge of creative expansion in the public sector. It was brought about because of a relaxation in the public monopoly, and because people saw opportunities for profit by introducing the new equipment.

In areas of the economy which are characterised by effective demand, rather than by compulsory supply, all kinds of different minds are working on ways of gaining advantage by offering new products and services to customers in novel ways. The order which results from the myriad of inputs is no kind of stable order; it is a dynamic order, the order which describes a continuing and ever-changing process.

It is more likely that successful solutions will be found where many are working on the problem, than where the energies of only a few are involved. In demand-oriented sections of the economy, it is the fact of the many creative talents which are engaged which leads to the greater frequency of successful innovations. It is not often in the economics of state-produced supply that a country can afford to back several solutions simultaneously, in order to see which one eventually develops the best economic potential. On the contrary, the decision is usually made centrally to commit to one type of solution.[8]

When demand rules, however, there may be several simultaneous solutions. In that people are different, and are satisfied by different things, it is quite possible that several types of product or service may survive simultaneously, each with its following of satisfied customers, each making money for its suppliers, and even with each changing, developing and improving under the continuous impact of innovative ideas.

There is no way of predicting the pattern of production and supply which will develop in response to effective demand. The creative innovations which will emerge to meet expressed or conjectured wants cannot be foreseen; in some cases chance itself plays a part in their development. Even the demand is unpredictable, let alone the novel devices employed to satisfy it. It would have taken a bold prophet to anticipate a year in advance of the event that large numbers of people would wish to while away the hours by manipulating a multi-coloured cube in the attempt to line up various coloured squares on separate faces, or that people all over the country would pit their wits and skill against cathode ray screen pictures representing invaders from outer space.

The habits of focussing on the supply side of the economy die hard. The unpredictability of supply in the demand-led areas comes to be a cause of uncertainty and suspicion. Legislators grow accustomed to thinking in terms of the allocation of resources to meeting production targets. They interpret the problem as being one of determining in advance the optimum use of inputs. Great effort goes into the selection of priorities, into the decision as to whether health should get more increased spending than education, or whether the coal mines merit a higher apportionment than do the recipients of social security.

The prospect of not making such decisions at all leaves both legislators and administrators staring into the void. How can they be sure about what form of supply would result? Would there be sufficient capital investment to produce it? Would the standard be high enough to meet needs? These questions, and many other similar ones, originate from the habit of a concern over supply. The same legislators never worry that record players will be available in the shops when they are needed, or that there will be enough capital investment to produce them. They do not worry that they would be available in the styles, colours, and quality demanded, and in suitable locations.

Record players are among the many items produced in a market led by demand, and which routinely deals with questions whose answers cannot be known in advance. The argument that record players are comparatively unimportant, and that different arrangements are required for essential items, is not valid. It may be true that record players are less important than health and education, assuming that some opinions about relative importance are to count more than others. What is not true is the supposition that public production guarantees the supply.

It is again a habit of supply orientation to suppose that something must be predictable to be guaranteed. Because we do not know what form the supply would take in a private market does not mean that it might suddenly disappear. After all, we can throw dice without knowing which number will come up, even while knowing that one *will* come up. Food is reckoned by many to be important, yet large areas of its production and supply take place in response to demand. We do not have to assume that baked beans might suddenly become unavailable unless their production is planned and controlled by government.

On the other side of the coin, it is equally fallacious to suppose that public production guarantees supply. The reverse is true: public production is the biggest threat to uninterrupted supply. If we look at items which the public has had to forgo at times because they were unavailable, we find that the list is drawn overwhelmingly from public sector goods and services. It has been electric power, coal, refuse collection, rail travel and publicly-produced steel which have seen supplies interrupted.

When an item is produced by public monopoly, its supply becomes concentrated. Those engaged in the production of it can, by strike action, deny the public access to it. The monopoly denies people the opportunity to turn to competing supply, and thus makes the strike effective. This is one reason why public sector goods and services meet the needs of the producers before those of consumers. It is a reason why it is to be expected, sooner or later, that an item produced in the public sector will have its supply interrupted.

Far from public production being needed to guarantee supply, it is the one thing which makes supply uncertain. Those engaged in the planning and administration of public supply fondly suppose that their plans ensure that supplies will be adequate. In fact their plans take place only within the established economic paradigm, and merely allocate such production resources as can be commanded or are thought appropriate.

All kinds of circumstances regularly conspire to thwart those fond suppositions. Demand changes unpredictably. There is a shortfall of raw materials. A strike results in a loss of production. Costs rise unexpectedly. All of these, and many more, are routine causes of the failure of public sector output to coincide with that intended. The fact that predictions are made for public sector supply leads to the illusion of control rather than the reality of it. The outcome is no more certain than it is for private production in response to demand; it substitutes an inaccurate figure in place of none at all.

The publicly-produced supply is not only denied the creativity which leads to demand being satisfied in all kinds of innovative and unpredictable ways, it is denied one of the most progressive mechanisms enjoyed by a demand-led market. If people are able to satisfy their demand by purchasing that which best meets their requirements, then the successful innovator has the incentive to undertake the risk. He gains not only the rewards of success, but the possibility of further creative action. The resources freely directed towards him through the purchase of the supply he produces provide capital for further development. His success also attracts others to share future risks with him, in the hope of sharing his gain.

The effect is to direct resources into the hands of entrepreneurs who have shown themselves successful at providing that which people want to buy, thereby accelerating the rate at which new ideas can be launched by those already proven successful at economic innovation. The public supply has no such mechanism; instead it is self-fulfilling. People buy what is produced because they have no choice; the purchase is made out of tax funds on their behalf, and monopoly usually prevents alternative choices. The supply is thus consumed in a way which forecloses any option of information being gained about what people want.

It could be argued that the public supply enables proper priority choices to be made. In a market led by demand, people might allocate less to health and education than the state spends on their behalf. By 'proper' priority choices, one refers to the allocation thought appropriate by legislators and administrators. It is indeed possible that people left to make their own decisions might make different allocations. The question arises as to why the view of the legislators and administrators should prevail. They know less about the circumstances of a person and his or her family, and they care less.

Evidence from non-public areas of the economy, and from countries which do allow private choice in such matters produces no evidence that people are less ready or less able to make sensible decisions on their own behalf, than their rulers would make for them. People seem to know how much they wish to spend on education, and how much on health; how much on housing, and how much on entertainment. They do, admittedly, show wide variation in their opinions, but the economy is capable of meeting that wide variation of demand with an equally diverse range of supply.

It is in the public sector that consumption is equalised, and that people are assumed to share the same supply requirements. If there are some small minority who would act irresponsibly towards their families, and spend on drink and horses what society thinks should be the minimum to go on food, shelter, health and education, the indicated procedure is to locate such persons and punish or constrain them, rather than adopt a procedure which denies choice to all on the grounds that some might abuse it.[9]

The foregoing discussion of the role which creativity plays in economic activity suggests that many of the problems which afflict large-scale public sector supply can best be solved outside it. It suggests that the most fruitful approach would be to set in motion forces which can conjure up their own solutions. If the demand is liberated and made effective, no-one can predict what kind of answers would be produced; but one can say that the conditions appropriate for inventive and innovative ideas would have been established.

Apart from the repeal of all monopolies which prevent alternative choices to public sector provision, the major incentive required from government is a reduction in taxation. It is the high level of taxation taken to support public sector activity which prevents effective demand for alternatives. The huge sums consumed to no good purpose by state industries as well as state services have to be funded from the resources which could otherwise be encouraging creative innovation in the administration and delivery of health care, in developing new ideas and techniques in specialist education, in providing new insurance initiatives for attractive options in pensions and social security.

There are other inhibitions on creativity, such as regulation and the obligation to comply with over-detailed rules. There are, on the other hand, many institutional procedures and arrangements which can be adopted to give innovation active encouragement. Limited liability to minimise risk of failure, with peerages and knighthoods to augment the rewards of success, are all factors working with economic creativity instead of against it, even though they undoubtedly represent state interference in economic processes.

It is taxation and monopoly, however, which exert between them a deadening force which is difficult to counter. They create circumstances in which an administration can be locked into a public sector spiral with no apparent way out. Because of lack of creative inputs, the public sector falls behind the progress which private industry makes in keeping pace with technology and advancing expectations. Added to its inflexibility, its producer-orientation and its chronic under-capitalisation, this creates pressure for something to be done. Taxation and monopoly keep consumers captive in the public sector to sustain that pressure.

The problem for government is that to spend more on the public sector means to increase taxation, either directly or by inflation, which locks it into another round of the spiral. Even worse, the higher public sector spending will cost more jobs in private industry and involve the administration in a higher payment for relief of unemployment.

One solution proposed to rescue an administration caught in the public sector spiral is that of a revenue-raising tax cut. The thinking is that lower tax rates will make it less worthwhile to evade and avoid tax liability, and will encourage people to earn more. Even with lower tax rates, runs the reasoning, a government can still gain a total tax yield which is greater than it was taking at the higher rates. This is the basis of the Laffer Curve, and what has been called 'supply side' economics in the US: the notion that a lower rate can generate a higher tax base to yield an increase in total revenue.[10]

The advantage of the proposal is that if it works it enables an administration to lower taxes, giving people more demand power to exercise on the creative side of the economy, while simultaneously raising the revenues needed to sustain the public sector and attempt improvements to it. If a government enters into Laffer Curve economics at a time when the economy has turned up from a recession, it is entirely possible that the tax cuts might accelerate an increase in tax base. The revenue available for investment and expansion is increased, as is that available to purchase the products. The increased production and sales could indeed provide a sufficient increase in taxable activity to offset the reduction in the tax rate. This would work, however, only at certain rates.

Any administration which embarked upon such a policy when the economy was heading down into a recession might find a different outcome. It is quite possible in such a case that the remitted funds would not find their way into increased production, but go instead to sustain activity which would have to be curtailed earlier without them. Firms on the margin would be able to survive longer; contraction of unprofitable activity could be postponed; labour could be retained which would otherwise have been laid off. The total effect could be one of delaying the descent into a recession, making the slope both shallower and longer. In such a case the administration would not make up its tax level by an increased base, and would incur a deficit. Deficit spending to ameliorate a recession is called by an older name.

A further criticism of the speculative tax cut is that, while an increase in revenue might solve the immediate problems of the administration, it is no good thing in the long term for a government to have more money to spend on the public sector. On this view, one feature of a successful solution is that it should involve a decrease in the proportion of funds consumed publicly.

An alternative approach, and one calculated to achieve precisely this effect, is to open loopholes in the public sector with the avowed intent of permitting demand to escape through them. Bereft of the innovation and development which appear in response to effective demand, the public sector becomes progressively less attractive to its captive consumers. Instead of attempting to redress this effect, or make it more acceptable, an alternative policy would encourage people to escape from it, to make them no longer captive.

The ways in which people would obtain an alternative and equivalent supply outside of the public sector need not be of concern to legislators. The fact of their demand would call into being some form of supply, some form which cannot be predicted in advance because it would be a creative response to that demand. Tax rebates and exemptions provide the means whereby those who leave through the newly-opened loopholes can take with them at least a part of the funding required to purchase the service. Even were they to take into the private market only the *saving* made possible in the public sector by their departure from it, a significant number would find this sufficient incentive.

The addition of numbers to the demand for supply outside of the public sector will lead to a build-up in the range and quality of services offered, and to the entry of more competition into the field, with new minds being brought to bear on possible improvements. This, in turn, will make the private supply even more attractive by comparison with its public equivalent, and lead to more exit through those loopholes. The option of going private will be taken down market, so it becomes not the prerogative of the few who can afford to pay twice over, but a normal choice within the range of most people.

As people see more and more of their contemporaries making the journey, especially those of equivalent status and living standard, they will be the more tempted to consider the option themselves. As the well-to-do are followed by the articulate middle classes and then by the skilled labourers, so those who exert greatest demand pressure on the public sector will lose any personal interest in supporting its high budgets.

The cumulative effect is to reduce the significance of the public supply and its deadening effect on the economy. Economic growth will take place not in the public sector, but in the equivalent and alternative services around it. Where demand stimulates economic creativity, there will the advances be made. Shorn of the usage which justifies and sustains it, the public supply will diminish as a proportion of the total, as governments find it ever easier to hold and reduce its allocation.

This solution to some extent involves duplication of resources and allowing public capital to be wasted as the population ceases to use it. This is no bad thing, compared with the present situation. Capital needs to be renewed periodically in any event, and some public sector stock could undoubtedly be transferred to the private sector and renewed there.

Lest anyone should suppose that this solution would be achieved at the expense of the less well-off, it should be pointed out that these are the main sufferers in the status quo. It is the poor who have to make do with the shoddy and inadequate public supply. The well-off can escape by paying twice, while the middle classes know how to use the system. The improvements and advances made by the encouragement of economic creativity would benefit the poor as well as the rich. It is the way of economic innovations that they work their way down the market. Whatever it is that is the prerogative of the rich when it is new, be it colour television sets or jet travel, shows a propensity to find its way to a mass market. There is no question but that the same would happen with the products and services now dominated by public sector supply.

There may be those who would need welfare support, perhaps by a negative tax, to command the necessary resources. There may be areas which people will prefer to leave in the public sector, such as catastrophic health insurance or chronic or geriatric care. But for the vast range of supplies which are produced at present within the public sector, there is little doubt that the trickle of persons who make alternative arrangements elsewhere could become a flood. With increasing numbers given the opportunity to leave, and with creative responses being elicited in the private sector by those increased numbers, a convergent process could be set up which culminated in the restoration of large segments of the economy to those areas governed by the discipline of demand, and subject at last to the innovation and invention which it elicits.

FOOTNOTES

1. See especially G. L. S. Shackle, *Imagination and the Nature of Choice*, Edinburgh University Press, 1979.

2. As well as those works cited in footnotes 1, 2, & 3, Chapter 1, see Ludwig Von Mises, *Epistemological Problems of Economics*, D. Van Nostrand, Princeton, New Jersey, 1960; Heinrich Rickert, *Science and History: A Critique of Positivist Epistemology*, D. Van Nostrand, Princeton, New

Jersey, 1962. Three brief and useful introductions to the Austrian School approach in general are Thomas C. Taylor, *The Fundamentals of Austrian Economics*, Adam Smith Institute, London, 1982; Alex H. Shand, *Subjectivist Economics: The New Austrian School*, Pica Press, n.p., 1981; S. C. Littlechild, *The Fallacy of the Mixed Economy*, Institute of Economic Affairs, London, 1978.

3. See Ludwig Von Mises, 'Comments About The Mathematical Treatment of Economic Problems' and B. Leoni and E. Frola 'On Mathematical Thinking In Economics', both in *The Journal of Libertarian Studies*, Vol. 1, No. 2, Spring 1977; and E. W. Streissler, *Pitfalls in Economic Forecasting*, I.E.A., London, 1970; B. McAndrew, 'The Failure of Economic Forecasting', *Policy Report*, Vol. 111, No. 11.

4. This argument is from Karl Popper, *The Poverty of Historicism*, Routledge and Kegan Paul, London, 1957.

5. See Sir Karl Popper, *The Logic of Scientific Discovery*, Hutchinson, London, 1959; *Conjectures and Refutations*, Routledge and Kegan Paul, London, 1963; *Objective Knowledge: An Evolutionary Approach*, Oxford University Press, 1972, and see also Madsen Pirie, *Trial and Error and the Idea of Progress*, Open Court, La Salle, Illinois, 1978, and Armen A. Alchian, 'University, Evolution and Economic Theory', *Journal of Political Economy*, Vol. 58, No. 3, June 1950.

6. See Kirzner, *Competition and Entrepreneurship*, op. cit, especially pp. 1-87.

7. For some interesting examples of the similarities between some economic analysis and biology, see Gordon Tullock, 'An Application of Economics in Biology', in F. A. Hayek, et al, *Toward Liberty*, op. cit., Vol. II, pp. 375-381; and Jack Hirshleifer, 'Economics From a Biological Viewpoint', *Journal of Law and Economics*, Vol. XX, No. 1, April 1977.

8. Regarding the idiocies and failures of various attempts at economic planning, forecasting, and nationalised enterprises, see John Jewkes, *The New Ordeal By Planning: The Experience of the Forties and the Sixties*, Macmillan, London, 1968; *Idem*, *A Return To Free Market Economics: Essays On Governmental Intervention*, Macmillan, London, 1978, pp. 53-76, 136-169; George Reisman, *The Government Against the Economy*, Caroline House, Ottawa, 1979, especially pp. 149-172; 'Spartacus', *Growth Through Competition: An Alternative To The National Plan*, I.E.A., London, 2nd edn, 1969; J. B. Ramsay, *Economic Forecasting - Models or Markets?*, I.E.A., London, 1977; J. Brunner, *The National Plan: A Preliminary Assessment*, I.E.A., London, 3rd edn, 1969; D. Burn et al, *Lessons From Central Forecasting*, I.E.A., London, 1965; M. Deaglio, *Private Enterprise and Public Emulation*, I.E.A., London, 1966; G. Polanyi, *Planning in Britain: The Experience of the 1960s*, I.E.A., London, 1967; G. Polanyi, *Short-Term Forecasting: A Case Study*, I.E.A., London, 1973; R.

Boyson, ed., *Goodbye To Nationalisation*, Churchill Press, London, 1971; G. & P. Polanyi, *Failing the Nation: The Record of the Nationalised Industries*, Fraser Ansbacher, London, 1974; *Idem*, 'The Efficiency of Nationalised Industries', *Moorgate and Wall Street Review*, Spring 1972; John R. Baker, *Science and the Planned State*, 1945, and reprinted in *Idem*, *The Freedom of Science*, Arno Press, New York, 1975; H. Schoeck & J. W. Wiggins, eds, *The New Argument in Economics: The Public versus the Private Sector*, D. Van Nostrand, Princeton, New Jersey, 1963; Georges Gallais-Hamanna, *Les Nationalisations . . . A Quel Prix? Pour Quoi Faire?*, Presses Universitaires de France, Paris, 1977; A. L. Chickering, ed., *The Politics of Planning: A Review and Critique of Centralized Economic Planning*, Institute for Contemporary Studies, San Francisco, 1976; F. A. Hayek, ed., *Collectivist Economic Planning*, Routledge and Kegan Paul, London, 1935; *Idem*, 'The New Confusion About Planning', in *New Studies in Philosophy, Politics, Economics and the History of Ideas*, Routledge and Kegan Paul, London, 1978.

9. In fact, the elitist view of well-to-do socialist intellectuals that the masses would not, for example, educate their children, is contradicted by historical evidence. As E. C. West has shown in his *Education and the State*, I.E.A., London, 2nd edn, 1971, even at the early stages of the industrial revolution, when the standard of living was still low and compulsory state education did not exist, parents were doing their best to purchase private education. Rhodes Boyson makes the same point in his *Crisis in Education*, Woburn Press, London, 1975.

10. The most concise account of supply-side economics can be found in Bruce Bartlett, *Reaganomics: Supply-side Economics in Action*, Arlington House, Westport, Connecticut, New York, 1980; See also Jude Wanniski, *The Way The World Works*, Simon and Schuster, New York, 1978, esp. Chapter 6, pp. 96–115; L. H. Meyer, ed., *The Supply Side Effects of Economics Policy*, Martinis Nighoff, The Hague, 1981; J. W. Middendorf II, 'A Walk on the Supply Side'; and B. Bartlett, 'Supply-Side Success Stories', both in *Reason*, Vol. 13, No. 3, July 1981.

Supply-side economics has not gone without criticism, however, from other economists of both libertarian and 'Austrian School' leanings. Thus, see Richard Ebeling, 'Supply-Side Economics: A Return to the Law of Markets or the New Indicative Planning', paper delivered to the Adam Smith Club, Westminster, London, December 1979. For a reply to such criticisms, see Bruce Bartlett, 'In Defence of Supply-Side Economics', *Manhattan Report* (International Centre for Economic Policy Studies, New York), Vol. 1, No. 7, October 1981.

A critique of practical privatisation

Few governments in democratic societies have succeeded in reducing the size of the public sector of their economies, although several have attempted to. The experience of the Conservative government in Britain of 1970–74 is a salutary one. Elected after the Selsdon Park proposals which promised to decrease the degree of state involvement in the economy, and return whole sections of state-owned assets to the private sector, the government succeeded, in its three-and-a-half-year term, in denationalising a small brewery in Carlisle and a travel agency.

During that period the commanding heights of the economy remained unscaled. State ownership of the mines and the railways was uncontested. The public utilities — gas, electricity and water – remained as state monopolies. Public services such as postal and telephone communications were as firmly in state hands at the end of the government's term as they were at the beginning. Throughout that period, for well over ninety percent of the population of Britain, there was no alternative to state-provided education or state-provided health services.

The exit from the public sector of a brewery and a travel agency was more than matched by the entry of Upper Clyde Shipbuilders and Rolls-Royce. The result was that the government elected in 1970 to increase the share of private enterprise in the economic process, left office in 1974 with a public sector substantially larger than the one it had inherited.

Naturally enough, observers have offered explanations to account for the strange gap between intent and performance. The obvious explanation which sprang to mind was duplicity. Although the Conservative opposition had promised denationalisation, it was argued, there was never any serious intention to achieve it. On the contrary, claimed some critics, the 1970–74 Conservative administration was managerial and opportunist, as others had been. While denationalisation had made a good rallying cry to arouse the faithful, once in office the government soon found the notion bore no practicality to the problems of the day.

An alternative, though similar, account has it that although the government was sincere in its promise, it soon changed its mind. Realising that doctrinaire commitment to free enterprise had no place in the modern politics of the 1970s, the government soon sloughed off its ideological skin, and moved towards the politics of the necessary.

Commentators of a more historicist bent have solemnly assured us that, although the Conservatives wished to advance the private sector, the inevitable progress of a modern economy into centrally-directed channels proved too strong an historical momentum to be withstood.

In all of these proposed explanations, private enterprise is accorded a role akin to that of the lost innocence of childhood. While it was charming and admirable in its day, it belonged to our youth, and is one of those childish things which must be put aside when one becomes a man. When economies, like individuals, grow up, the immature stages of their infancy may be looked back upon wistfully, but never restored.[1] The Selsdon Park proposals are to be seen as a yearning for that lost childhood, rather than a serious programme for progress in adult life.

While this analogical fallacy has the advantage of enabling private enterprise to be dismissed as childlike naivete, instead of having to be dealt with on a rational level, it fails, unfortunately, to provide a model of the actual process of defeat.[2] Given a new government with a parliamentary majority to back up its commitment, and administrative experience to support its intentions, how is it that Inevitable Historical Destiny, or dawning adulthood, or whatever it was, managed to set itself between the aim and its fulfilment?

Some critics, to fill the gap which would otherwise be left by the exigencies of the times, or the movement of historical progress, have alleged that the failure was one of will. The government of the day, sound though its intentions may have been, was simply not tough enough to override the forces of inertia which acted against it. The implication of this analysis is that a subsequent government, more resolute and forceful, can succeed where the 1970–74 government failed, if only it acts more firmly.

This theory, too, has its weaknessness, not the least of them being that while several personality failings were ascribed to the prime minister of the day, lack of will was never one of them. A more serious objection is that a failure of resolution can always be used as an explanation for any failing of government. If an apparently tough and determined government can be accused of lack of will for its failure to cut the public sector, the explanation appears to tell us only that no government perhaps is tough enough to do it. One can live in hope that some government, some day, somewhere, will be sufficiently resolute; or one can look at the institutional and political forces which influence, among other things, the will of government.

An altogether more simple explanation of the performance of the government of 1970–74 is that it wanted to cut the public sector, but was unable to do so. It was not equipped to deal with the public sector inertia which is set against those who attempt to transfer some of its goods and services into the private sector. Nor was it equipped with any of the sophisticated and subtle techniques which are required to overcome that inertia. Like so many other governments, it appeared to assume that will and power were sufficient, and in consequence neglected technique.

The performance of the 1970–74 government in Britain is now a matter of historical record, but the public sector problems which it threw into relief remain. While people may favour a transfer to the private sector in general and in abstract, the four groups involved in any particular section of the public sector all have a strong motivational interest in its retention.

The legislators, nominally at the top, may go through specific phases committed to putting more state-directed resources into private hands, but their long-standing pressures lead them in the other direction. The stock-in-trade of legislators is involvement and regulation. Their business is the business of others. They gain their support by deciding where the balance shall lie between competing claims. To expect them voluntarily to surrender control of an area once subject to their detailed supervision is to expect the unusual. Circumstances and needs may occasionally conspire to produce a government which contracts the area of its authority; the reverse is the normal.

The administrators who direct the state concerns have nothing to gain by having their responsibilities removed. On the contrary, their career structure and remuneration have been calculated to reward those whose area of authority is enlarged, rather than diminished.

On the labour side, both the workforce and the union officials feel themselves threatened by the prospect of denationalisation. The workforce, it is true, would gain by being employed in a thriving and adequately capitalised private business; but they would certainly lose the ability to negotiate working agreements which place their own comfort and convenience above that of the consumers of the goods or services provided. The union officials would certainly lose both power and authority, since private employers are harder to deal with than governments worried neither by loss of business nor bankruptcy.

The public at large, who might be expected to constitute the main beneficiaries of the transfer of state concerns to the private sector, identify themselves lukewarmly as producers, but keenly as consumers. Each public sector offering has a devoted coterie of enthusiastic beneficiaries, but only vague and distant opposition from those who provide its costs. Thus, even though far more might gain if a service went private, the few who oppose the move will be more vigorous and more visible. Each public service therefore puts pressure from its beneficiaries, through the media, to the legislators; while no identifiable interest group balances them in support of the general good.

Any successful policy to reduce the domain of collectivised provision must be one which takes account of the pressures from these four groups, and which either diminishes them or overcomes them with superior pressures generated elsewhere. In the absence of any such accounting, the administrators, the labour force and its unions, the beneficiaries and their spokesmen and dependents will all ensure that pressure is put on the general public, and through them, the legislators, to stop or at least reduce the movement out of the public sector.

Classification of goods and services

The various techniques employed to move goods and services out of the public sector may be inspected within the context of a fourfold division of economic activity. Since goods and services may be produced publicly or privately, and paid for publicly or privately, we can allocate them into four quadrants.[3]

Goods and services in Quadrant 1 constitute the traditional public sector, in that they are both produced and paid for publicly. Such things as police services, state health and education occupy this quadrant, being produced by persons directly employed by the state, and paid for by governments out of revenues collected through various forms of taxation.

Quadrant 4 represents the private sector, and features such things as food, clothing and electrical goods. Produced in the private sector and paid for privately by consumers, its items are subject to market pricing and competition.

	Produced publicly	Produced privately
Paid for publicly	1	3
Paid for privately	2	4

Fig. 1.

The goods and services in Quadrant 2 are those which are paid for by a charge upon users or purchasers, even though they are provided publicly. In Britain such services as the provision of gas and electricity fit into Quadrant 2, whenever they more or less pay for themselves out of user charges. Telephones and some self-supporting municipal transport services provide further examples.

The remaining section, Quadrant 3, is occupied by the goods and services which, although paid for out of public funds, are nonetheless produced in the private sector. Much of our defence equipment comes into this category, including ships, missiles and tanks which are manufactured by private enterprise, but commissioned by the government and paid for out of taxation.

Many of the techniques of privatisation and denationalisation attempt to move goods and services directly along the diagonal from the first quadrant to the fourth. In order to bring more of the economy within range of the disciplines and benefits of market forces, proposals are made to lift parts of the public sector directly into the private domain.

One such proposal involves the direct sale of state assets. Where a discrete and viable section of the public economy can be separated off and put up for sale, there is the prospect of direct transfer to the private sector, with the price compensating the public for the loss of its asset. The potential owners represent an interest group in favour of the transfer, so the more widespread the ownership, the greater the built-in support.

In cases where diffuse ownership, gained perhaps by a flotation of shares, is inappropriate, the sale might be made to the labour force. This neutralises the potential opposition of one of the four groups, for the workforce can stand to gain more by owning the enterprise than it gained by remaining in the public sector.

There is a Catch-22 drawback to the sale of state assets. It is that a profit-making industry need not be sold, and a loss-making industry cannot be sold. Certainly, any government which waited until public enterprises moved into the black, and then waited for the right market conditions to unload them onto the private sector, would find itself waiting a long time and unloading only a little. A brewery and a travel agency would count as a good score, given those preconditions.

The dilemma can be confronted by an equally formidable beast composed of the same elements: a profit-making industry can easily be sold, and a loss-making one *must* be sold. Part of the solution to the problem of moving state enterprises along the diagonal from public to private lies in creating a class of beneficiaries of privatisation. One way of achieving this is to dispose of state assets at a discount, such that the purchaser makes a capital gain on the purchase to offset against any short term loss on the current account.

Council housing provides a good example of this technique. To compensate tenants for the loss of below-market rents and free maintenance, the houses are offered for sale at a price below valuation. Thus, although by purchasing the buyer will pay more for accommodation, he will have acquired a capital asset worth more than he paid. A new class of beneficiaries of privatisation is created in this way, and assists the process of transfer.[4]

In a few cases of loss-making public enterprises, it may be possible to give away the industry concerned to some group, perhaps its own workforce, which has the prospect of making it pay. Faced with the certainty of their privileged position being ended, they might prefer this to the alternative. The 'public asset' so disposed of appears to be of doubtful or negative value, in that all the state loses is the obligation to meet continuing losses. In some cases there is the prospect of giving the industry to the public at large which already owns it in name. In this so-called 'Volkswagen' solution, shares are issued to the public as confirmation of their stake in this publicly-owned operation. Now that each citizen has his or her individual piece, however, it can be used to vote in company elections or policy decisions, and can be alienated. The company has been put into private hands simply by putting into the hands of the public which owns it.

In a large class of state undertakings which have for too long been run as subsidised public services rather than as commercial activities, there may be no prospect of sale or gift to place them in the private sector in the immediate future. For such concerns, the prospect of partial privatisation might present itself as a step upon the way. If all of the enterprise cannot be denationalised, perhaps a part of it can. Alternatively, if part of it cannot be wholly privatised, perhaps the whole of it can be partially privatised.

If parts of the industry can be packaged as economic units, there is the possibility of their transfer to the private sector. Failing this, there is the alternative possibility of devising means whereby private capital can be attracted to, and involved in, an industry which remains for the time being under state control. The involvement of private risk capital in road-building, railway modernisation projects, or civil engineering, offers the chance of bringing in some of the advantages of market disciplines. A systematic application of such a policy would diminish the proportion of public capital in the industry, and take it almost imperceptibly into the private sector. In the meantime, of course, the policy enables reinvestment and re-equipment to take place without increase to the public sector of the economy.

Non-diagonal transfer

While all of the methods of denationalisation discussed thus far involve moving completely or partially along the diagonal from Quadrant 1 to Quadrant 4, there are in addition several possibilities of non-diagonal movement. For cases in which there is no possibility of any movement directly towards the private sector, the suggestion has been made that transfer of the method of payment into the private sector is an important move in itself, quite apart from the prospects it offers for subsequent transfer of the production into private hands.

This method, involving as it does the charging of individuals for public goods and services, transfers the activity from its public sector Quadrant 1 position into Quadrant 2, where public sector production is financed through private user charges.

The argument is given that it is public finance which is responsible for many of the failings of the public sector. With no price inhibitions on use, and no capitalisation based on measured need, both quantity and quality of supply tend to be based on political factors instead of on economic or commercial ones. If the public have to pay directly for the service, claim the advocates of charging, then their demand is restrained by price. They have the choice, moreover, of not consuming and not paying. Their own allocation of resources will determine the appropriate supply of service, and price can be fixed at a level which will ensure the meeting of future needs.

Furthermore, the argument runs, once the public is paying privately for a state service, and the enterprise has to run as more of a commercial undertaking, it will not be a difficult matter to complete the denationalisation by taking the state production into the private sector. Charging thus offers the prospect of taking state activities into the private sector by an anti-clockwise, rather than a diagonal, movement, and one which takes us first into Quadrant 2.

While this approach is undoubtedly better than no movement at all towards the private sector, there are several serious criticisms which can be made. If production stays in the public sector, especially as a state monopoly, then none of the disciplies of competition is introduced. There is no incentive to control costs, to implement more efficient working methods, or to keep up to date with new technology and capitalisation.

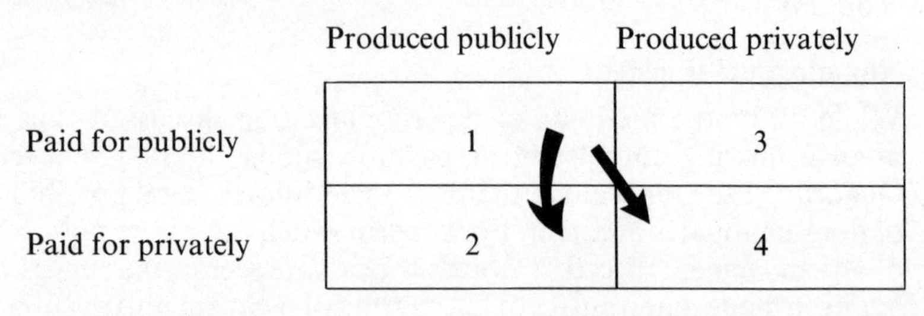

Fig. 2.

The imposition of user charges to replace direct finance from public funds involves the legislature in the determination of price. Even if the charges are fixed by an independent body, they will be subject to review and confirmation by legislators at local or national level. Inevitably, this involves the legislators in a process which makes them vulnerable to pressure by interest groups. The annual determination of the charge will provide occasion for a variety of lobby groups to demand below-market prices, and for legislators to experience the downward pressure from interest groups, with none of the counter pressure from the population generally which benefits more from economic charges for services.

The attempted route to privatisation via charging, in other words, leads to a situation in which there are all of the disadvantages of public sector monopoly production, combined with constant pressure to keep the charges at an uneconomic level. Legislators who favour private, rather than public, enterprises are made very vulnerable. A public sector production with in-built cost escalators is combined with a system of user charges for which legislators are ultimately held to be responsible.

Far from providing a momentum towards a totally private sector service in Quadrant 4, the move into Quadrant 2 creates an unstable situation which tends to reverse itself. The pressure is not from private method of payment to private method of production, but from private method of payment towards public method of payment. The tendency is towards uneconomic, non-market charges, subsidised out of taxation. The standing trend will favour the election of legislators who will vote for tax support of user charges; and the charges themselves will tend to meet an ever lower proportion of the costs of the enterprise.

In cases where complete transfer to the private sector is not possible, a radical alternative to charging has been put forward. In this proposal it is the production, rather than the pricing, which is transferred into the private sector. The enterprise is moved from Quadrant 1 into Quadrant 3, and is now produced by private business, even though still paid for out of public money. In this clockwise movement through the quadrants, the public authority ceases to produce the service directly by in-house labour, but instead contracts with private firms to have the services produced according to agreed specifications.

As with charging, this partial move to the private sector offers the eventual prospect of complete privatisation. Once the production is in private hands, it is argued, with all that this entails, it is a short step to cut out the legislature's role as middle man, and allow the public to pay the contractors directly. Contracting out thus presents yet another alternative to the direct diagonal transfer from public to private sectors. The clockwise movement, leading first into Quadrant 3, is made in the conviction that it is more advantageous to privatise the production first, then the method of payment, than to attempt it the other way round, as charging does.

Consider the advantages of taking production into the private sector. In the first place it is almost invariably cheaper to have any given goods or services produced in the private sector. A collection of empirical data from all over the world has the public sector charging slightly more than twice as much as its private sector equivalent. Called by a variety of names at different times, a definitive version is Savas' Law, and stipulates that for a given service, the private version will cost 40% of the cost of public sector provision.[5]

The fact that the service cost is reduced is a major incentive to the legislators who seek ways of reducing public expense, and the public which pays it. The private service is probably also more efficient. Coming to it *de novo*, the private contractor is encumbered with none of the history of working practices which characterised the public service. There will be less visible misuse of public resources. The private service will probably be better than the public one it replaces. The private contractor needs to keep up to date with what can be offered, or he risks losing the deal to a competitor.

The private service will usually be more modern, and more capable of retaining a high standard of service. The contractor has to keep abreast of changes in his field, or competitors will replace him. He has to keep up his capital investment, and is not subject to the forces which lead public services to eat into their capital programmes in order to finance higher current expenditure. Curiously enough, even the quality of service is easier for the public authority to keep up if it is performed by an outside business and can be measured objectively by the authority's personnel against contractual requirements.

Given all of these cost and service advantages, once the legislators have taken the decision to privatise the production, both they and the public stand to gain. The two remaining groups, namely the administrators and the labour force, enjoy no such immediate advantages; incentive schemes provide a means for public authorities to convey benefits to these two groups as well, thereby cementing the change. Administrators have a higher grade of service as contract monitors to provide job opportunities and a means of enhancing status and salaries, while the workforce should be hired preferentially by the new contractor at higher basic rates with better perquisites and status. Union officials may still be in opposition, but with so many beneficiaries of the transfer, a sufficient counterforce is produced to outweigh them.

There remain, of course, the disadvantages of public sector finance. The public, when not paying directly, will often demand a quantity and quality of service out of all proportion to that which they would be prepared to finance if they realised that their own money was involved. Against this may be set the downward pressure on cost brought about by competitive tendering.

Contracting out services appears to be a relatively stable movement out of the public sector. Experience provides few cases of public authorities which move back to public sector production after experience with contractors, and many cases of authorities which go on to privatise more of their services after a successful experience with the first.

There is the possibility opened up by contracting out of transfer to private finance after successfully transferring to private production. Once the efficiencies of private supply are at work, it is quite possible that extra services may be offered to those prepared to pay more, or that some may be permitted to contract out of both the service and the payment. Both of these are examples of gradual movement towards private finance, completing the clockwise movement through the quadrants.

	Produced publicly	Produced privately
Paid for publicly	1	Contracting out 3
Paid for privately	2 Charging	4 The private sector.

Fig. 3.

Local government services provide fertile ground for privatisation achieved by contracting out to private business, while retaining, for the time, at least, payment out of public funds. Refuse collection and disposal stands out as an obvious candidate, being easily measured and costed; but one could add street repair and maintenance, all types of building repair and restoration, the cleaning of public buildings, catering, transport, security, parks and gardens and leisure facilities.

All of these services have been put out to contract for provision by private enterprise by local authorities somewhere in the world.[6] Not only these, but the technical work of local government departments, including the work of architects, solicitors and town planners, has been successfully provided on a contract basis. Even social welfare has been privatised in this way, with individual families contracting to look after the elderly in their own homes, or to take problem children into their households.

The ultimate in seeking local services from private production has probably been reached by one county in California, in which the local authority meets periodically to award all local services out to competing contractors, and even has the work of monitoring the performance of the businesses concerned handled by an outside, private agency.[7]

There are areas within the public sector nationally which could be taken into Quadrant 2 successfully. The provision of ancillary health services, such as the cleaning of hospitals and the catering performed within them, could incorporate the benefits of private sector production, even though financed under contract from public funds. The cleaning and maintenance of public buildings, including railway stations, could go to private firms, as could most public sector catering. Examination of the public sector reveals everywhere parts of it which, even though perhaps unsuitable for immediate transfer to the private sector, could have their production side taken there.

The cumulative effect of all of this clockwise movement through the quadrants is to increase the economic activity which takes place in the private sector, at the expense of that which is performed collectively by employees of government. Whereas anticlockwise movement, or charging, does not necessarily effect any significant reduction in public sector production, it does at least give people more control over the allocation of their resources. Both are useful gains, although the latter is much more vulnerable to gradual reversal.

Whether transfer to the private sector takes place along the direct diagonal, or in a clockwise or anticlockwise direction, the selection of the most suitable mechanism to effect that transfer can be made only after close study of the system at the level of individual motivation. The four groups which participate in public economic activity — the legislators, the administrators, the workforce and the consuming public — must be seen as sections which will act quite rationally to maximise their self-interest. If this self-interest for any group lies in the retention and increase of public sector supply, it should come as no surprise to find that their actions tend to produce that outcome.

Privatisation can be achieved through mechanisms which will direct the self-interest of these groups towards private sector supply. Conditions must be created institutionally which lead individuals to support this transfer for their own advantage, and which lead to their gaining more from the transfer than they will willingly afterwards relinquish.

In cases where it is not possible to do this for all of the groups involved, it may be possible to create perceived self-interest among some of them strong enough to outweigh the continuing opposition among the others. It may even be appropriate, in some cases, to provide direct financial compensation to the groups whose benefit must be foregone. In nearly every case the long-term gain of transferring goods and services to the private sector will more than make up for the short term loss incurred by the payment.

The financial and economic calculations are insufficient. It is entirely possible that the most sensible project of denationalisation will fail to be carried through because insufficient attention has been paid to institutional and political considerations. It is not lack of will which makes governments fail in their attempts to reduce the size of the public sector of the economy. It is lack of knowledge and lack of expertise.

FOOTNOTES

1. Like so many socialist arguments against freedom, we find this argument usually riding in uneasy harness with an opposite, but equally anti-libertarian, assertion. We are told that economic freedom was viable in the early stages of growth, but impossible or undesirable in an advanced or complex society. At the same time we are told that the problems of the

undeveloped and primitive economies of the Third World necessitate socialism and planning. On this point see Murray N. Rothbard, *Power and Market*, op. cit., pp. 174–175.

2. It is also historically illiterate. There is no inevitable or even actual tendency. History reveals societies at countless different industrial and technological levels, divided between those with statist, authoritarian, or collectivist systems and those with more libertarian ones. It is the latter which have prospered, supplying the masses with material and social advancement. It is the more market-oriented nations of the West, and of Asia (eg. Hong Kong, Japan, Malaysia etc.) which prosper, rather than the barren and sterile areas blighted by the myriad variants of socialism. Socialism represents a regression to the primitive authoritarian systems which caused so much of humanity to stagnate and suffer in the past. See, for example, Louis Baudin, *A Socialist Empire: The Incas of Peru*, D. Van Nostrand, Princeton, New Jersey, 1961. See also Arthur Shenfield, *Myth & Reality in Economic Systems*, Adam Smith Institute, London, 1981.

3. This distribution of goods and services appears in John Burton, 'Making the Delivery of Public Goods More Effective and Less Costly': paper delivered at Windsor Castle, 10 June 1981.

4. See Murray N. Rothbard, 'Buy Out The Obstructors', *Journal of Economic Affairs*, Vol. 1, No. 3, April 1981, on the importance of this sort of strategy.

5. See Professor E. S. Savas and Barbara J. Stevens, *Evaluating The Organisation of Service Delivery: Solid Waste Collection and Disposal*, Columbia University Graduate School of Business, New York, 1971, Savas found that, in a survey of 2,000 cities of 250,000-plus population, a municipal twice-weekly garbage collection service cost 69% higher than privately contracted services. See also, Mark Frazier, 'Privatising the City', *Policy Review*, No. 12, Spring 1980, p. 100.

6. For general analysis and evidence for this argument see Robert Poole, Jr, *Cutting Back City Hall*, Universe Books, New York, 1980, passim. The rather misleading titled work by William C. Wooldridge, *Uncle Sam The Monopoly Man*, Arlington House, New York, 1970, also contains much interesting evidence on the private provision throughout history of those services which people incorrectly assume can only be supplied by the state. Brief general discussion and evidence can also be found in Michael Forsyth, *Re-Servicing Britain*, Adam Smith Institute, London, 1980; Mark Frazier, 'Privatising the City', *Policy Review*, op. cit.; Jarret B. Wollstein, *Public Services Under Laissez-Faire*, Society For Individual Liberty, Silver Springs, Maryland, 1969; L. H. White, 'Privatisation of Municipally-Provided Services', *Journal of Libertarian Studies*, Vol. 2, No. 2, Summer 1978; Robert Poole, Jr, 'Contracts: Key To Urban Rebirth' and James Q. Wilson, 'Rent-a-Sheriff: Market Control of Public Services' in *Reason*, Vol. 4,

No. 1, April, 1972. A number of the major works produced by the contemporary anarcho-capitalist school also provide much empirical data on privatisation — as well as urging the total privatisation of governmental functions. Thus, see M. & L. Tannehill & J. B. Wollstein, *Society Without Government*, Arno Press, New York, 1972; Murray N. Rothbard, *For A New Liberty*, Collier-Macmillan, New York, 2nd edn, 1978, and David Friedman, *The Machinery of Freedom*, Arlington House, New Rochelle, New York, 2nd edn, 1978.

7. In a regular column 'Trends', the American magazine *Reason*, has described countless examples of privatisation. To document my assertion the reader should see

Prisons and Rehabilitation of Criminals: Rehabilitatory and manufacturing facilities at Lino Lakes, Minnesota, Vol. 11, No. 1, May 1979/Vol. 9, No. 6, October 1977. The former chief programme administrator of New York's Department of Correctional Services has also urged the privatisation of prisons, see Vol. 10, No. 2, June 1978. Experimental private rehabilitatory schemes instituted in North Carolina, Maine, and Indiana, Vol. 5, No. 3, August 1977.

Weather Forecasting: The National Weather Service observation team at Washington National Airport has been privatised, Vol. 11, No. 10, February 1980.

Entire Public Works Department: Including garbage collection, street cleaning, snow removal, and road repair, in Utica, New York, Vol. 8, No. 2, June 1976.

Courts: Contracting out the public defenders' function (i.e., legal aid defence) in the Los Angeles County Court system. Also, in California, many companies bypass the state court system entirely and settle cases by private courts and arbitration, Vol. 12, No. 9, January 1981.

Roads: In West Houston, a group of land developers, corporations and other private financial interests have, following the rapid urban growth, constructed their own private freeway (i.e. motorway), Vol. 12, No. 3, July 1980.

Police: Various federal government agencies in the USA have turned over virtually the entire protective/security functions to private contractors. Vol. 13, No. 3, July 1981. Lexington, Kentucky, has hired private police for patrolling high crime areas, with great success. Munich, West Germany, is also using private security forces in high crime creas, Vol. 7, No. 10, February 1976. Orangeville, Toronto, in Canada, also wished to privatise its entire police department, but was stopped by Federal law, Vol. 4, No. 4, August 1972. In San Francisco, police patrols are operated — and have been from 1899 — on a semi-privatised, customer-financed basis. For a detailed account see C. Durffi, 'San Francisco's Hired Guns', *Ibid.*, Vol. 11, No. 4, August 1979.

Garbage Collection: Privatised in St Paul and Minneapolis, Minnesota, and Wichita, Kansas, Vol. 7, No. 10, February 1976. Also in Milwaukee, New Orleans, and Portland, Oregon. For a more detailed analysis, see K. Peterjohn, 'Dumping the Garbage Monopoly', *Ibid.*, Vol. 12, No. 7, November 1980.
Ambulance Services and Paramedics: Privatised in a number of Californian cities including Santa Barbara County and Glendale; Vol. 7, No. 10, February 1976. Ontario's provincial Department of Health also privatised its Health Care Services in Halton County, Vol. 4, No. 4, August 1972. In Louisiana's Gulf Coast there also exists an entirely private enterprise ambulance service, the Acadian Ambulance Service, Vol. 6, No. 5, September 1974.
Data Processing: Orange County, California, privatised its data processing operations, serving some 25 County agencies, Vol. 6, No. 2, June 1974.
Airports: A wholly private enterprise airport constructed and operated by Northrop Airport Developments Corporation at Bangkok, Thailand.
School Services: Private day care centres hired by Dade County, Florida; school cafeteria contracted to McDonalds in Benton, Arkansas; certain students sent to private schools for special courses in Grand Rapids, Michigan; Vol. 8, No. 7, November 1976. There have also been 40 different experiments in the USA during 1975 for 'performance contracts' with private enterprise in education, Vol. 7, No. 10, February 1976. In Gary, Indiana, Behavioral Research Laboratories has been given a four-year $2.6 m contract to take over Bannecker Elementary School — the company must refund the per-pupil cost for any child in the 6th grade who fails to reach or exceed national norms in reading and maths, Vol. 3, No. 12, March 1972.
Fire Brigades: The fire brigade in Scottsdale, Arizona, has been privatised with great success since 1952. Following its success in this town the Rural/Metro Co. has expanded its services into Georgia, Tennessee, and Rochester, New York.
Welfare: An experimental private family placement project has been tried in Kent. See Sir John Grugeon, 'Better Welfare Services at Lower Cost' in *Economy and Local Government*, Eamonn Butler & Madsen Pirie, eds, Adam Smith Institute, London, 1981; also A. Seldon, *Charge*, op. cit., p. 183. On private welfare in the USA, and for suggestions on privatising state welfare by tax credits, see D. J. Devine, 'Welfare Without Injustice', *Modern Age*, Vol. 21, No. 2, Spring 1977, pp. 167–169, 170–171.
Parks and Recreation: Some parks and recreation facilities privatised in San Francisco; landscaping and park maintenance privatised in Arlington Heights, Illinois, Vol. 8, No. 7, November 1976.

Conclusion

I have attempted, in this short work, to cast doubt on the whole basis of the public sector of the economy. The use of central power to collect information, make decisions and deploy resources accordingly is an ingrained and substantial part of the economy of all advanced countries. Analysis shows, however, that despite its entrenched position, the public sector is subject to serious anomalies.

Much of the information needed by government as a basis for public sector decisions is too diffuse to be of value, too low in accuracy to accomplish what is sought of it, or too much concerned with our own indices and constructs to tell us about economic reality.

Governments not only base some of their decisions on information about unreal aggregates; they also neglect quite often the realities which stand against their activities. A lack of readiness to consider the motives for self-advancement among legislators, administrators and public sector union officials can lead to complete misconceptions about the possibilities of success in public policy.

The logic of economics, even while pinpointing the anomalies which enter attempted economic management on the large scale, directs our attentions instead to the microeconomic level, where the information needed for individual action has not been scattered away, and where motivation is admitted as the major factor in the calculation. The same logic points us away from a preoccupation with large-scale supply of public goods and services, and towards measures which can set an effective demand to call forth its supply in response.

It is the irrationality inherent in public supply economics which thwarts the intentions of those who employ it, turning an ostensible aim to serve the public with goods and services into an achievement which serves the producers. The same failure to conform with economic logic gives us a public supply which is expensive and inadequate, which employs high-cost labour and yet allows its capital to run down. It gives us the inflexible service which pre-empts the funding for a better one. It gives us the standard service, while squeezing out the creative processes which could improve it.

There are measures which can be employed by a government in pursuit of economic objectives, and with the expectation of success. These are those which look to demand, and to ways of enabling the preferences and priorities of people to be met on an individual basis, rather than by mass production of what is construed centrally as the appropriate supply. Privatisation of the public sector is a part of that answer; encouraging demand for alternatives to public sector supply is another part. Without doubt there will be further parts forthcoming.

If the public sector is not to dominate and distort the entire economic process by its use of resources, its concentration on producer needs, and its denial of creative opportunity, then its re-orientation to a concern with demand is long overdue.

Index of Proper Names